Christmas
IN THE KEY OF G

by Karen Lail

Trilogy Christian Publishers
A Wholly Owned Subsidary of Trinity Broadcasting Network
2442 Michelle Drive Tustin, CA 92780

Rights Department, 2442 Michelle Drive, Tustin, CA 92780.

Trilogy Christian Publishing/TBN and colophon are trademarks of Trinity Broadcasting Network.

For information about special discounts for bulk purchases, please contact Trilogy Christian Publishing.

Trilogy Disclaimer: The views and content expressed in this book are those of the author and may not necessarily reflect the views and doctrine of Trilogy Christian Publishing or the Trinity Broadcasting Network.

Manufactured in the United States of America

10 9 8 7 6 5 4 3 2 1

Library of Congress Cataloging-in-Publication Data is available.

ISBN: 978-1-64773-670-5
E-ISBN: 978-1-64773-671-2

To the praise, honor, and glory of

God the Father,
The ultimate giver of all good things;

God the Son,
the reason we celebrate Christmas;

And God the Holy Spirit,
Our encourager and intercessor.

Thanks be to God!

ACKNOWLEDGMENTS

Family is one of the greatest blessings God gives us, and I have certainly been blessed with mine. Thanks first of all to my parents, Roger and Phyllis, who encouraged my earliest scribblings. I miss you every day, Dad, and Mom, after all these years, you are still one of my greatest cheerleaders!

To my children, Melissa, Phillip, and Kelsey: It's amazing to look back at all the life changes that have occurred since I first started writing this book—most notably the addition of a daughter-in-law and two grandchildren to our ever-growing family. I am so proud of each of you!

To my first readers—daughter, Melissa Lail Zinn, and sisters in faith and Best Friends at Work (BF@W), Brenda Sartori and Kris Beech: Thank you for your time, honest feedback, and steadfast encouragement. This book is as much a result of your efforts as mine, and I am deeply grateful.

To my niece, Jessica Van Eseltine of Jessi V Photography: I enjoyed the time we spent trekking through the field and down by the pond to take the photo that graces the back cover. Thank you so much for sharing your time and talent!

And, finally, to my husband Terry: I cherish the love story we've been writing daily for the past thirty-five years. Thank you for believing in me.

CHAPTER 1

Monday, December 3rd
Los Angeles, CA

Thumbs hooked in his front jean pockets, Gideon stood outside a row of tidy shops and looked up and down the sidewalk impatiently. *Where the devil is he?* Gideon slowly, silently counted eight beats and, calm again, pulled his cell phone from the inside pocket of his tan corduroy sports coat. *Ten past three.* He looked from side to side again, but there was still no sign of his brother. *I did get the address right, didn't I?* He scrolled to Gareth's message and reread it:

> SECRET MISSION: Meet at Chandler's
> Jewelry Store 1237 Crispin Street @ 3 PM.
> TELL NO ONE! Thanks Bro!

Gideon twisted slightly to glance at the street sign—corner of Crispin and Nicholas—and looked back up at the store name. Yes, this was the right shop: Chandler's Jewelry, Family-Owned Since 1955. *How in the world did Gareth know about this place?* Most stores in L.A. tended to the modern and edgy or to the ubiquitous Spanish style, but this quiet street with its shops of gabled bay windows, black half-timbering, creamy white stucco, and brick painted in pale gray had an Old World type of charm.

Gideon pressed Call. After a brief ring, his brother's voicemail greeting sounded: "Hi, it's Gareth. Please leave me a message."

"Hi, Gareth, it's me—again. I'm still waiting for you. Call me."

The storefront window sign, encircled by greenery and white twinkling lights, caught his eye as he ended the call: "Let us help you design her custom engagement ring this Christmas!" The activity around him seeming to fade, he smiled down at the picture of the lovely blonde-haired, brown-eyed girl that served as the wallpaper on his phone. *Trish*. He looked again speculatively at the sign as he pocketed the phone. He and Trish had only been dating about eight months, but this would be their first Christmas together as a couple—and the first time in years that he and his family would actually be home for the holiday season. He was anxious to take their relationship to the next level, but of late Trish had been... well... contrary.

His smile faded. Contrary. That was an understatement. Yesterday she'd texted to suggest they take a break from dating, but he'd asked her to hold off until he could see her later that evening, convincing her to forego the party they were scheduled to attend and instead just spend the time talking through their differences. She'd been a little standoffish, almost sullen when he'd first arrived at her apartment, but by the end of the evening, she had warmed up to the point that they could even laugh together. But no matter how encouraging last night's conversation had been, Gideon knew there was still a lot to work through.

No, until they could get on the same page about where they were headed as a couple, this wasn't the time to think about getting her a ring. "Maybe for Valentine's Day," he murmured.

Cl-clang!

Flinching, Gideon spun, lowering into a defensive crouch, his fists clenched and held ready to strike out.

Eyes locked with Gideon's, the sidewalk Santa who had been tolling a hand bell with emphatic flicks of the wrist, stopped mid-peal, hands and bell held up in mock surrender.

Gideon smiled sheepishly, relaxing his stance as he straightened, and with an answering twinkle of his blue eyes, Santa lowered his arms as well.

"Sorry about that," Gideon said, fervently hoping no one had captured the scene on camera. What a headline *that* would be: "Gideon Locke Assaults Santa". He repressed a shudder and reached into his back pocket.

"It was my fault. I sometimes get a little carried away with the bell," Santa confessed, "but there's nothing that says Christmas more than bells and chimes."

He broke into a relieved smile. "I agree," he answered, removing a couple of five-dollar bills from his wallet and placing them in the collection pail suspended from a tripod.

Santa beamed at him. "Thank you! Merry Christmas!"

Gideon's phone pinged. "Merry Christmas. Excuse me," he replied absently as he took out his phone and studied the message from Trish, his smile fading with growing dismay.

> Hi. I know we had a really good talk last night, but I've been giving it a lot of thought and I think we should just call it quits. To be honest, Marcus says I need to focus on people who can actually help me with my acting career. It was fun being with you, but you and I both know that we want different things. So goodbye, Gideon.

He was thunderstruck. What had happened to the commitment she'd made last night to working things out?

His jaw tightened. *Marcus.*

Gideon glanced back at the jewelry store, the sign in the window flashing mockingly. To think, just moments ago, he'd been thinking about their holiday plans.

About when he might give her a ring…

Too bad we won't be going to Vegas or Tahoe or some other tourist town for the next few weeks after all.

His phone pinged again as another message from Trish came through:

> PLEASE don't hate me.

Don't *hate* her? Why would she think he'd hate her? Hurt that she wasn't as committed to their relationship as she'd led him to hope, yes. Frustrated because, once again, she'd caved to her agent's wishes. A little peeved that she'd taken the coward's way of breaking up. But *hatred?*

Shaking his head dazedly, he exited the message. No, the only one he really held a grudge against was Trish's agent, Marcus Webber. Ever since Trish had signed on with him, Marcus had been manipulating and reshaping her until Gideon never knew which version of Trish would greet him when he picked her up for a date: the sweet, adventurous girl who had first caught his eye, or, more often of late, the pseudo-sophisticate who made it clear she found him a bore.

Oh, Trish.

"Girlfriend running late?" Santa asked sympathetically.

Snatched back to the moment, Gideon looked at Santa, really noticing him this time. "No... no girlfriend." Once again, he added to himself as he stuffed the phone back inside his coat. "I'm waiting for my youngest brother, Gareth, actually. He asked me to meet him here but he's late again, as usual."

"He probably got held up in traffic. I'm sure he'll be along soon."

"I hope so," he said with a dismissive nod as he started to turn away.

Santa's next words arrested him.

"So are you and your brothers performing anywhere over the holidays?" Chuckling at Gideon's chagrined expression, Santa continued, "You may think that blond wig is a disguise, but *I* recognized you. You're one of the Locke Brothers. Since you're not Gareth, which one are you: Gabriel, Graham, or... Gideon?"

He knows exactly who I am. All the brothers were similar in appearance, having light brown hair, dark brown eyes, their mother's slightly upturned nose, their father's square jaw. But there were distinctive differences. Gareth's hair had natural golden highlights. Graham wore his hair a little long and sported a close-trimmed beard to hide the red birthmark on his jawline just below his left ear. Gabriel, who had inherited his father's sturdier bone structure and had struggled with his weight as a child and young teenager, was now the most

Karen Lail

muscular of them all. Gideon, in his mind, was identified by what he did *not* have: He did not have blond highlights, he did not have a beard or birthmark, and although he had ripped abs and well-developed muscles too, he did not have the brawny wrestler's build of his oldest brother.

Recovering the aplomb all his years of being in the public eye had instilled, Gideon flashed his "camera smile" as he grasped Santa's hand. "I'm Gideon, the third brother." And then he froze. *Is this really a Santa's helper or just another reporter in disguise?*

Santa seemed unaware of Gideon's uneasiness. "Ah, yes—the drummer. So what have you and your brothers been up to?"

Gideon's anxiety fled, leaving him almost weak with relief. *No reporter worth his salt would ask a lame question like that.* "Performance-wise, things are on hold for a couple of months. Graham and his wife Shannon are expecting their first child in January."

"That's right—I remember hearing about that. It's an exciting time."

"Yeah. And even though we're not performing this holiday season, we're already rehearsing for a six-week gig in April. We're also writing some songs and we're even planning a new album."

The thought of the new album brought another pang. Trish was supposed to go to the record label's Christmas party with him next Friday. Obviously, *that's* not happening. *I wonder if Rachel's sister would mind stepping in as my plus-one again.*

"I'm glad to hear that. I've always enjoyed your music."

"I never realized Santa was a fan of ours," Gideon said lightly.

"I don't fit the typical demographic for a Locke Brothers fan, do I?" he acknowledged with a beam. "I've been keeping tabs on you for quite a few years—all part of my job, you understand."

"Oh, of course," Gideon agreed, enjoying this bit of whimsy.

"So now that both Gabriel and Graham are married, I take it things aren't quite as hectic as they were in past years?"

"It's definitely not the whirlwind that it used to be—we can actually catch our breath a little between venues. And the audiences are not as... well... fanatical."

"Yet you still wear a wig out in public," Santa pointed out gently.

Gideon felt an unexpected flash of anger. *Who was this guy to poke at him for wearing a wig?* Reining in his temper, he said with a terse smile, "Let's just say that sometimes it still gets crazy when people recognize me."

Santa nodded sapiently. "What you mean is… there are still some girls who hope to snag one of the famous Locke Brothers."

"*Or* use us as stepping-stones in their own careers," he added bitterly, Trish's text fresh in his mind. "So, *yes*, I still wear the wig," he ground out.

Santa reached up and stroked his natural white beard. "You could always try facial hair."

Gideon laughed, his good humor restored. "I doubt I could carry the look off as well as you do."

"You may have a point," Santa conceded with a smile. "But seriously, if you weren't an entertainer, what would you *want* to do?"

Struck, Gideon replied, "That's funny—no one has ever asked me that." He thought for a minute. "I did the online degree thing, and that was fine, but it wasn't the same as actually being on a campus. So I'd go back to college, preferably on campus but online again if necessary, and get my teacher certification—probably in music education, since that's what I know and love."

"That makes sense. After all, you're the one who taught Gareth how to read music." Seeing Gideon's questioning look, he added vaguely, "Oh, I heard that somewhere."

Gideon cast his mind back over all the interviews he'd given through the years. Funny, he was sure he hadn't mentioned that fact in any of them. Maybe Gareth had. Yes, that was more likely.

Santa smiled and thanked the pedestrian who had slowed her pace long enough to drop a couple of coins in the pail before hurrying on. He turned his attention back to Gideon. "So you'd want to be a music teacher," he prompted. "What else would you want besides experiencing campus life?"

"I'd want to see what a *normal life* is like, whatever *that* is—a life that doesn't involve endless interviews and so-called parties, weeks of being on the road, or being chased by paparazzi." He looked at Santa self-consciously. "And, hopefully, find someone who loves me for

Karen Lail

who I am, not *what* I am or what doors she thinks I can open for her."

"I've heard lots of impossible wishes over the years, but believe me, there's no reason why yours can't come true."

Gideon shrugged. "I used to believe that. Now—not so much."

"I realize that your line of work makes it hard for you to be a college student in the traditional way and yet… Maybe you could visit some college campuses the next time you go on tour and get information about their online teacher certification programs."

"That's not a bad idea."

"And as for love…" He placed his free hand on Gideon's shoulder. "Remember the old adage: Good things are worth waiting for?"

Gideon nodded.

"Trust me, I know," Santa continued. "I was thirty before I found my wife." He paused for a beat and then added, "It's hard to find a woman who doesn't mind living at the North Pole year-round."

Gideon chuckled.

"The point is, Gideon, love doesn't have a timetable, and not all girls have a hidden agenda. You may even discover that some of them have been hurt as badly as you. Just be patient—you'll find her." Looking past Gideon, Santa lowered his arm and added with a twinkle and a lift of his chin, "And speaking of patience, I think your brother is coming now."

Turning, Gideon saw Gareth dashing towards him.

"Sorry I'm late," Gareth said, hunching over and resting his hands on his knees as he regained his breath. "Traffic coming across town was a nightmare."

Santa flashed an I-told-you-so smile at Gideon before turning away to resume ringing his bell.

"Not a problem. Are you okay?" Gideon asked, noticing his brother's labored breathing.

He nodded. "Instead of trying to hunt for a parking place close to the store," he replied, beginning to breathe easier, "I decided to just go to the parking deck about three blocks away. I ran all the way here."

"No wonder you're out of breath. So what's this 'secret mission' that you need my help with? Why are we *here*?" he asked, gesturing to the store name.

"Rachel's father told me about this place when I talked to him last night." He straightened up, meeting his brother's eyes, his expression a curious mix of determination and pleading. "He gave me his blessing. I'm going to propose to Rachel on Christmas Eve."

Gideon was stunned. He knew things had been getting serious between them, but *marriage—already?* They were barely twenty-three.

And then another thought reared its head: *It should have been me.*

A crisp ring of Santa's bell snapped him back to the moment. Seeing the mix of hurt and puzzlement on Gareth's face, Gideon realized his brother had interpreted his silence as disapproval. Banning all self-pitying thoughts from his mind, he forced his lips into a smile as he reached out and tousled Gareth's hair. "That's wonderful, bro. I've always thought you and Rachel were a perfect couple. But surely you don't need *my* help to propose to her, do you?"

His relief palpable, Gareth grinned as he smoothed his hair. "Of course not. What I *would* like your help with is picking out a ring."

"Oh, Gareth, that's something you and Rachel should choose together. Why don't you wait until *after* you've asked her? She may have something very specific in mind."

"No, I have a good idea of what she'd like. Besides, I really want to surprise her with the ring when I propose—just like in all the classic movies. You know: the hero pulls out a ring box and drops to one knee… the whole nine yards." He put his hand on Gideon's shoulder. "And who better to help me than my favorite brother—who I hope will also be my best man?"

"Really? You want me to be your best man?"

"Of course! You've always been more than my brother. You're my best friend—next to Rachel, of course."

Although Gideon was actually closer in age to Graham than he was to Gareth—Graham and Gideon were just nineteen months apart, as opposed to the three years and eight days that separated Gideon and Gareth—he and his youngest brother had formed a special bond almost from Gareth's birth. Over the years, that allegiance had counterbalanced the alliance Gabriel and Graham had forged long before Gideon had been conceived.

"I'd be honored, Gareth. But about this ring…" He shifted uncomfortably.

Gareth dropped his hand back to his side and waited.

Santa moved, drawing Gideon's eye, and nodded encouragingly at him.

Gideon's eyes cut to Gareth again. "If you're sure you want to do this without her, I'll help you."

Gareth's wide smile creased his face. "You will?"

"Yeah," he said, clapping his brother on the shoulder and walking with him to the double doors of the store. "Let's do this!"

The peal of Santa's bell greeted them when the brothers emerged from the jewelry store about an hour later.

"The timing couldn't be more perfect!" Gareth said gleefully, reaching for his wallet. "I can pick up the ring on the eighteenth and have it all ready to give to her on Christmas Eve."

"Sounds like a plan," Gideon responded as his phone pinged. "I'm really happy for you, Gareth. And I'm sure Rachel will love the ring you chose." He pulled out his phone and checked the screen while Gareth deposited a bill in Santa's pail with a nod and a smile. "It's Dad. He's going to be late getting home tonight." He raised his eyes to Gareth's. "Hey, why don't we grab a bite and watch Monday Night Football to celebrate your coming engagement?"

"I'd love to, but Rachel and I have plans for dinner and a movie. Why don't you and Trish join us?"

Gideon shook his head slightly, avoiding Gareth's gaze. "Yeah, that's not going to happen."

With sudden understanding, he said, "She dumped you, didn't she?" At Gideon's reluctant nod, Gareth eyed him with concern. "Why didn't you tell me?"

Gideon smiled ruefully and held up his phone. "It happened just before you got here."

"You mean she couldn't even do it in person? Tell me she at least *called* to break up with you." Seeing his brother look away again, he laid a hand on his arm. "Oh, Gideon, I'm sorry. I'll bet picking out a ring was the *last* thing you felt like doing today."

Gideon snapped his head back to face Gareth. "No… no, you're wrong. It was good to have something else to think about. It's even put me in the mood to do some Christmas shopping of my own."

"Are you sure?"

"Yes, I'm sure. In fact, it's the perfect time to get *your* present since *you'll* be out of the way," he said with a grin, tucking his phone away again.

Laughing, Gareth wrapped his hand around Gideon's thumb and pulled him in for a one-shoulder hug. "Thanks again for your help."

"My pleasure."

With a grin and a wave, Gareth charged off in his headlong way, but then spun around, walking backwards, arms outspread. "Who knows? Maybe this time next year I can return the favor!"

"Yeah," Gideon said, watching his brother turn and nimbly side-step a couple laden with shopping bags. His grin faded. "Maybe."

Behind him, Santa smiled and continued to ring his bell.

CHAPTER 2

Friday, December 14th

Hepton Grove, NY

Situated approximately thirty-five miles west-northwest of Lake George, New York, the town of Hepton Grove nestles near the base of the Adirondack Mountains. Named for Erastus Hepton, who in 1731 had first settled the region with his sons, Amos and Josiah, Hepton Grove had expanded to an area of almost four square miles by the time it was incorporated as a township in 1867. Twenty years ago, the town was in danger of fading into obscurity, but today it covers just over ten square miles—nearly eleven including the homes located outside the town limits but still serviced by the Hepton Grove post office—and bustles with renewed vigor.

Although the municipal website boasts the availability of two good-quality hotels and a lovely bed and breakfast, the travelers who venture to Hepton Grove are few. Typically, those who do cross into the town limits come, not by their own devising, but because they waited too long to book a room at the popular tourist destinations of either Saratoga Springs or Lake George, and therefore must widen their search for lodging. Nevertheless, over time a number of those involuntary visitors have been so captivated by the town's setting, history, and unapologetic conservatism that they ended up relocating there permanently, with the result that the array of goods, services, and specialized practices available in Hepton Grove now rival those of much larger municipalities.

It is a charming town, characterized by wide streets—some of which are still outlined by their original brick pavers—built around a central court square, where residents and visitors gather for seasonal celebrations, outdoor concerts, and other events. Although the original Hepton homestead was lost to a fire at the beginning of the 19th century, fine examples of colonial, Greek Revival, and even Second

Empire architecture still remain in the town's historical district.

It is a town that, as of the most recent census, 9,803 souls—including the seven members of the Glencoe family—proudly and fondly call home.

———————————

It was quarter past six in the evening—nearly an hour and a half since darkness had settled over Hepton Grove—and one by one the shops and businesses along Main Street were closing for the day. Interior lights winked off, now here, now there, leaving the storefronts lit only by the reflections of street lamps and holiday lights. The windows of Glencoe Ophthalmology, however, remained brightly illuminated, and in the larger central suite, which jutted some eight feet closer to the sidewalk than the staff and examination wings that flanked either side, the placard on the front door declared the practice was still open.

Mallory Glencoe pulled the receipt from the printer and leaned across the reception desk towards the six-year-old girl who stood holding her mother's hand. "I love your new glasses, Lily."

She beamed. "Me, too. They're my favorite color!" She turned her head to one side. "And look—they've got *diamonds!*" she said, pointing to the purple earpiece.

Mallory exchanged a smile with Lily's mom before looking back at the little girl. "Wow," she replied, "your mom and dad must love you very much to buy you glasses with *diamonds.*"

"Uh-huh. Mommy said they're *special.*"

"They sure are," Lily's mom said, accepting the receipt from Mallory. "You need to take good care of them, don't you, Lily?"

Lily nodded solemnly.

"Well, say goodbye to Miss Mallory. Daddy is waiting for us."

"Okay. Bye, Miss Mallory."

"Goodbye, Lily. 'Bye, Mrs. Payton."

Mallory returned Lily's wave as Lily followed her mother to the door. Mrs. Payton waited patiently while Lily painstakingly zipped up her coat. Humming along to the strains of "O Come, All Ye

Faithful" playing over the speaker system, Mallory turned back to her computer.

A few moments later, Mrs. Payton and Lily exited the office. Caught by a wintry gust, the door snapped shut after them with a protesting clang of the sleigh bells that hung from the door handle. Sensing movement behind her, Mallory swiveled to her left.

"Seriously? Again?" she muttered, eyeing the wayward length of plump garland drooping from the peak of the wide arched doorway that separated the reception area from the optical department. Turning back to her desk, she pulled open the top right drawer, rummaged through the contents, and triumphantly held up a large paper clip. She crossed to the arch, dragging one of the waiting room chairs behind her, and with a tug on the right leg of her black dress pants, stepped up on the chair seat. Twisting the wire firmly, she closed one end of the paper clip around the garland and looped the other end over the small nail that protruded from the high-gloss white molding.

"Well done," an elderly male voice said approvingly.

Mallory glanced down with a victorious smile. The last patient of the day, eighty-year-old James Wyatt, stood next to her older brother, Aidan, in the archway leading from the examination rooms. "Thanks."

The chair wiggled as she reached to fluff the garland.

"Be careful, sis," Aidan warned, tucking a clipboard under his arm as he rushed forward and steadied the chair.

Mallory finished adjusting the garland to hide the nail and paper clip and then, resting her hand on Aidan's shoulder, stepped nimbly down to the floor. Leveling a minatory glare at her in response to the saucy look she tossed at him, Aidan handed her the clipboard and moved the chair back into position.

Mr. Wyatt chuckled. "That takes me back. Aidan always was protective of you," he said as he walked with Mallory to the reception desk.

It was true. Nine years separated the siblings, and Aidan had taken his role of big brother seriously—so much so that often during her teen years Mallory had complained that she had three parents instead of only two.

"Yes, and she has no more appreciation for it now than she did when we were kids," Aidan retorted as he joined them at the desk.

"Less," she replied impishly, winning a chuckle from both men. She removed the encounter sheet from the clipboard and nudged the computer mouse, bringing the monitor to life.

"Mallory will set up your surgery appointment," Aidan said, gripping his patient's hand warmly. "Thanks again, Mr. Wyatt. I'll see you soon."

"Thank you, Aidan," he replied with a nod as Aidan moved past him into the Staff Only wing. He drew out his debit card and then looked around the reception area while Mallory typed busily on the keyboard. "I've said it before and I'll say it again: Your parents buying these three stores and converting them into their office was the best thing that happened to our town."

Over the years, Mallory had heard similar comments from other patients, crediting her parents for sparking the wave of revitalization that had swept over the business district of the town in the latter half of 2001. Since then, downtown Hepton Grove had again become a thriving cluster of businesses and local government offices.

"Well, this town has been good to us, too," she answered. "Is next Friday morning at 8:30 all right?"

"That will be perfect. I'll be glad to get this out of the way before the end of the year."

"All right. We've got you scheduled for next Friday at 8:30 a.m. in Lake George. You'll need to arrive by 7:30, and someone will have to be with you to drive you home. And no food or drink after midnight," she cautioned. He nodded his understanding. "It's thirty dollars for today's visit."

He inserted his debit card and typed his 4-digit PIN on the keypad in front of him. "I hear your twin is coming home from his ski trip today. Colorado, wasn't it?"

"Yes, that's right," she said, making a notation on the encounter sheet and placing it face-down on the small stack on the credenza behind her. She handed the receipt and the appointment card to him. "All this snow around us and Max has to go to Colorado to ski—go figure," she laughed, locking her computer screen and rising from her desk.

"I guess the grass is always greener—or in this case, the snow is whiter?" he quipped as he folded the receipt and tucked it with the appointment card into his wallet.

"I guess so," she agreed, walking with him to the front entrance.

Mr. Wyatt settled his fedora on his head and lifted his coat from its hook on the wall rack. "When does his flight get in?"

"He was supposed to land at about three-thirty this afternoon. Phoebe drove to Albany to pick him up." She glanced at her watch. "They should be coming any time."

"I know you'll be glad to have him home. Will all of you be coming to the church Christmas party tomorrow?"

By "all of you" he means me, she thought. She *had* come to the party last year, but after just a few minutes had retreated to the sanctuary, where she'd sat huddled in a pew for the rest of the evening.

She lifted her gaze to meet his. "As far as I know, yes."

"Good." He tipped his hat to her. "Well, goodbye, Mallory—and tell your mother it's good to see her back at work."

"Thanks, Mr. Wyatt, I will."

The sleigh bells on the door jingled merrily as Mr. Wyatt left. Glancing over her shoulder, Mallory saw with satisfaction that the garland remained in place.

Turning back to the door's glass panel, Mallory made sure Mr. Wyatt navigated the ramp down to the sidewalk safely before she locked the door. She flipped the placard sign from Open to Closed, lowered the Roman shade, and then returned to her desk. Unlocking her computer screen, she printed the report of the day's receipts, stapled the pages together, and then launched the daily file back-up. With practiced ease, she removed the cash tray from the center drawer, folded and placed the report on top, and balanced the tray on her left arm while she picked up her key ring and the stack of encounter sheets for the afternoon's patients. She carried her burden through the archway leading to the examination area and unlocked the door to what they still referred to as the medical records room but, since the patient records had been fully digitized, now served as the computer server room and vault. Minutes later, the cash tray had been secured in the safe, ready for Phoebe to balance and prepare Monday's bank deposit, and the patient encounter sheets had been locked in the sole file cabinet pending the next quality assurance review and insurance billing. Mallory switched off the light, exited the room, turned the key in the lock, and tugged and twisted the handle. All secure.

The opening bars of "Little Drummer Boy" sounded from the speakers. Singing along softly, she dragged the black elastic ponytail holder from her hair and slipped it on her wrist as she walked back to her chair. She tidied the desk surface, made sure the drawers were pushed in all the way, and picking up her key ring again, locked the desk. She stopped singing when she heard a child's giggle from behind her.

They must have come in while I was in the records room, she thought with a smile. Eagerly, Mallory rose from her desk, walked through the archway leading to the staff offices and break room, and leaned against the open doorway of her parents' office. She watched in amusement as her father—still garbed in his white lab coat with *Roger Glencoe, Eye M.D.* embroidered above the breast pocket—spun slowly in his chair, first to the right and then to the left, as he held his five-year-old granddaughter Cassidy in his lap. It was an after-hours tradition that had started soon after Aidan, who was also an Eye M.D., had moved back to Hepton Grove with his wife and daughter to join Roger and Meredythe's practice. Roger and Aidan handled the more in-depth eye exams, treatments, and surgeries; Aidan's wife Phoebe was the business manager, and Meredythe had recently returned as the on-staff optometrist/optician.

Aidan, who had removed his own lab coat and was shrugging into his black wool topcoat, stepped out of his office and stood beside his sister. "She never gets tired of that," he said, his eyes fixed on his father and daughter.

Meredythe nodded her agreement as she looked on indulgently from the recliner that Roger had recently purchased for her to use as needed during the day.

"Well, one day she will… but I hope it's not for a long time yet," Roger said, stopping the chair's motion and planting a kiss on the crown of Cassidy's blonde head before lifting her from his lap.

"I thought Phoebe and Max were here, too," Mallory said in confusion, watching as Cassidy skipped over and grabbed Aidan's hand.

"Phoebe called me and said they were held up in rush hour traffic on the Northway, so I ran out and picked up Cassidy from after-school care," Meredythe replied, not quite able to keep the weariness from her voice.

"Oh," Mallory said.

"They should be here any minute," Aidan added.

Mallory bent down to her niece with a smile. "You look so cute—just like a little elf," she said as her gaze roved from Cassidy's black boots, her green leggings dotted with tiny white snowflakes, up to the white top with green rick-rack trim.

"That's exactly what *we* said when we saw her," Meredythe remarked as Cassidy giggled.

"It's the perfect outfit for visiting Santa," Roger agreed with a wink at his granddaughter.

Cassidy looked up at Aidan, her expression suddenly hopeful. "Daddy—" she began, but broke off and spun when the sleigh bells on the front door jingled again. "Mommy! Uncle Max!" she cried, dashing off to greet the couple who had just come in. Aidan gathered up Cassidy's coat, hat, and scarf and trailed after his sister and parents into the waiting room.

The family resemblance between Mallory, Aidan, and their father, Roger, was strong—all three had blue eyes and varying shades of auburn hair, from Roger's silvery copper to Mallory's glossy mahogany locks. Max, however, had inherited his mother's gray eyes and near-black hair. The spiky shortness of Meredythe's pixie cut made the similarity between mother and son even more striking.

"Mommy, are we going to see Santa tonight?" Cassidy asked eagerly as the others took turns hugging Max.

Phoebe bent forward slightly, protectively holding the bulge of her womb. "Actually, Daddy and I are going out for a while this evening. Mallory and Max are going to take you."

Max linked his left arm through Mallory's and, with a flourish of his right hand, pulled her down with him into a theatrical bow. "The Wonder Twins, at your service, milady," he said melodramatically, alluding to Max and Mallory's favorite childhood cartoon superheroes-in-training.

"You're a nut," Mallory laughed, brushing her hair back with her left hand as she disengaged from Max.

"I wish *I* had a twin," Cassidy said as Aidan helped her with her coat. "But I guess a baby brother will be okay."

Mallory put her arm around Cassidy. "It'll be *great*," she said, giving Cassidy a squeeze. "And just think: even though Max and I are twins, he's still my baby brother because *I* was born first."

"And you'll never let me forget that, will you?" Max said with a grin as he took her coat and scarf from the coat rack and handed them to her.

"Not a chance—it's one of the few things I can hold over your head."

"Well, maybe if you had *grown* a little more, you could hold *more* things over my head," he teased, comparing his six-foot-two build to her five-and-a-half-foot frame.

Meredythe rolled her eyes. "Here they go again," she said in an aside to Roger.

Her husband nodded. "Maybe *we* should take Cassidy instead. At this rate, the store will be closed before they get there."

"That's okay, Grandma and Grandpa—I've got this." Cassidy took hold of Mallory and Max and tugged them towards the door. "*Come on.*"

"I think that's our cue," Max commented to his sister. He pulled the door open. Exchanging farewells with Roger and Meredythe, Aidan and Phoebe led the way outside, followed by Cassidy, Mallory, and Max.

Aidan stooped down to talk to Cassidy. "Be good for Aunt Mallory and Uncle Max," he admonished gently as he pulled her hat more snugly over her ears and tightened the scarf around her neck. "You've been a good girl all year long—you don't want to mess up just ten days before Christmas," he added, touching the tip of her nose lovingly.

She giggled. "I won't, Daddy."

"That's my girl." He looked at his siblings as he rose and slipped his arm around his wife. "Thanks again, guys."

"Yes, thank you," Phoebe echoed.

"Is it okay if I leave my gear in your car?" Max asked his sister-in-law.

"Of course. It will probably be about nine o'clock, though, before we get to the house."

"Not a problem. I won't need anything before then."

"Have a great time, you two," Mallory said.

"But I bet *we're* going to have more fun than *you* guys, because *we're* going to go see *Santa*!" Max proclaimed, swooping Cassidy up and placing her on his shoulders.

Max can make everything an adventure, Mallory thought fondly, wishing yet again that she had inherited just a thimbleful of his big personality.

With final cries of "Goodbye," they parted from Aidan and Phoebe and headed up the street, calling greetings to neighboring shopkeepers and admiring the display of Christmas lights, wreaths, garlands, and bows on each building they passed: Carson's Bakery, Fulbright Insurance, the public library, the town hall, the fire station where even the grille of each fire truck sported a wreath… But when a couple about Max and Mallory's age exited Allison's Café and approached them hand-in-hand, Mallory suddenly turned and reached up to retie one of Cassidy's shoes as the couple exchanged hellos with Max.

"Hi, Mallory," the young man said, peering around Max to look at her.

"Jackson," she answered stiffly, not quite making eye contact.

"You remember Lindsey?" he prodded.

Mallory glanced over her shoulder as she tightened the bow. *Lindsey Fletcher? Really?* She patted Cassidy's foot before moving to face the couple. "Of course."

Lindsey leaned in closer to Jackson, placing her other hand possessively against his chest. "Hi, Mallory."

"We're going to see Santa!" Cassidy announced, unconsciously saving Mallory from having to respond.

"That's great," Jackson answered. "Have a good time," he added with one last look at Mallory as he let go of Lindsey's hand only to slip his arm around her waist instead.

"We will!" Cassidy sang out. Max raised a hand in farewell, but Mallory merely nodded with a tight smile.

"You okay?" Max asked softly.

"I'm fine," she answered with false brightness. She looked up at Cassidy. "We're almost there, Cassidy. Have you thought about everything you want to ask for?"

"Yup! I want *everything!*"

"Spoken like a true five-year-old," she said. This time her smile was genuine.

As they reached Prescott's Department Store at the corner of Main and Second streets, Max set Cassidy down. Laughing, the three of them crammed into the open wedge of the revolving door and pushed to enter the store.

A wonderland of delight stretched out before them. Crystalline snowflakes of graduated sizes cascaded here and there, and bright red cardinals roosted in the birch and white-flocked pine trees that stood sentry near each aisle and counter. Clutching Max and Mallory's hands, Cassidy swiveled her head from side to side while they rose up the escalator to the second floor, stepped off, turned, and then took the next escalator.

Max looked around as the escalator crested at the third floor. "We've been coming to Prescott's since we were—what, six?" he asked Mallory as they stepped off with Cassidy.

"That's right—we moved here in June, started kindergarten at the end of August, and turned six in November."

"Wow, it's hard to believe this is our twentieth Christmas in Hepton Grove!"

"I know."

"Well, all I can say is, in all the years we've been coming to Prescott's, it seems like their displays keep getting better and better.

This is just awesome!" he said with delight.

"Aw, I think there's still a six-year-old Max in there somewhere," Mallory said, poking at his chest.

Max grinned. "Come on," he urged, leading them to the line of children and adults waiting to see Santa. As they joined the queue, Max again looked around him with pleasure, then glanced down and noticed the pensive expression on Cassidy's face. "Cassidy, are you all right?"

She looked up at him. "Uncle Max, why are *you* and *Aunt Mallory* taking me to see Santa 'stead of Mommy and Daddy?"

Mallory looked at her in surprise. "But, Cassidy, I thought you *wanted* to see Santa!"

"I do. It's just weird that *you* had to take me *tonight*. Mommy and Daddy could have taken me tomorrow."

The twins exchanged a look, Mallory hiding a smile as Max bent down conspiratorially to his niece. "Maybe it's because Mallory and I want to ask Santa for something, too, but we felt silly coming by ourselves."

Cassidy looked from Max to Mallory and back again. "Really?"

"Really." He unzipped his black ski jacket. "See, I even wore my special red-and-green 'Visiting Santa' shirt."

"But what about Aunt Mallory? She looks like she always does— all gray and black, like she's sad."

Noticing Mallory's stricken face, he tried to think of a response that would lighten the mood again. His gaze dropped to his sister's neck. "You know, I think I have a solution." He twitched Mallory's cream-and-gray Nordic patterned scarf from around her neck and replaced it with his solid green one. He and Cassidy studied the effect of the green scarf against Mallory's charcoal-gray wool coat. "What do you think?"

Cassidy nodded. "I like it! It's much more Christmas-y."

"That's exactly the word I was thinking!" he said, giving her a high-five.

Mallory looked down at the scarf and then scanned the crowd around them. Although she recognized many children and adults from church and her family's practice, quite a few strangers—perhaps from neighboring hamlets—had come to Prescott's tonight, too. *Don't look at them!* her mind screamed. One arm held tight in front of her like a shield, she fingered the scarf self-consciously with the other hand as she stared ahead, oblivious of Cassidy's chatter. Each time Max and Cassidy moved forward, she would follow—mechanically, unseeingly. At one point Max leaned into her slightly and whispered, "Relax." With a guilty start, Mallory nodded, dropped her hand, and cast a swift look about. The line had snaked around so that they were now facing the people in line behind them. She turned to one side to avoid looking at them and again trailed blindly each time Max and Cassidy stepped forward.

"So what about *you*, Aunt Mallory?" Cassidy's voice piped from beside her.

Mallory twisted slightly to look down at her niece. "Hmmm?"

"Uncle Max said *he* wants to ask Santa for something. What about you?"

"Oh—absolutely!"

"Then you can go first," she replied mischievously, moving back a couple of steps.

"What?"

"That's very nice of you, Cassidy," Max said approvingly as he spun Mallory to face forward.

Somehow they had already reached the head of the line, and a glorious Santa's Workshop rose up against a backdrop of midnight blue that spread across the ceiling and down the top third of the back wall. Lights in varying shades of green and blue shimmered and shifted against the dark ceiling, mimicking the Aurora Borealis. A few elves sporting white lab coats and protective goggles were in the Testing area of the workshop. Some were running trains, flying remote-control drones and planes, or checking the rolling action of pull toys while others made notations on a clipboard. In the Packaging area, a couple of elves placed toys in brightly colored gift bags, which they then set on a conveyor belt. Further down in the Loading area, more elves took the packages off the conveyor belt and stuffed them in a large canvas sack in the back of a huge sleigh. Santa himself sat in an elaborately carved chair, positioned so that he could super-

Karen Lail

vise the activities in the workshop. Perched on a stool next to him, a female elf remained ready to help children in or out of Santa's lap or to soothe them if they were timid. Off to one side, another elf stood behind a digital camera mounted on a tripod.

Eyes riveted on Santa, Mallory hissed in a panicked whisper, "Max, it's not Mr. Guthrie."

"Careful," he said in her ear, pointing to the top of Cassidy's head. "It's okay. Go ahead, sis—he's waiting."

Feeling conspicuous, Mallory moved forward slowly. Santa beamed and beckoned her welcomingly as he murmured something to the elf next to him. The elf sprang up and, gesturing with both hands, motioned her forward and directed her to the stool—like a ground crew member guiding an airliner to a Jetway, Mallory thought. Embarrassed, she sat down gingerly and met Santa's kind gaze.

"Welcome, Mallory," Santa greeted.

Her body relaxed. Hepton Grove was rather a small town and most of the townspeople were patients of the practice. *I guess this Santa is someone I know after all.* "I'm really sorry to take up your time. My brother and I brought our niece here while her parents are out shopping. She got a little suspicious, so we told her *we* wanted to visit you, too," she explained with a sheepish laugh. "And," she said, with a ta-da gesture, "… here I am!"

"Well, I'm glad." Santa nodded towards Max, who was talking and laughing with Cassidy. "So Max is your twin brother, and Cassidy is your older brother, Aidan's, child?"

Mallory's smile diminished. Maybe this wasn't someone she knew after all. "Yes, that's us—the Glencoe clan."

"I hoped you would come by."

Mallory fidgeted uncomfortably, but remained silent.

"So, tell me, what would you like for Christmas, Mallory?" Santa prompted.

She gave a nervous laugh. "You don't have to ask me that."

"But that's part of my job: to find out what young people want."

"That's for children—not for… not for people my age."

"You let me be the judge of that. So what would you like?"

She shook her head as she shrugged. "I can't think of anything."

"Are you sure?"

She shook her head again, smiling shyly.

"Is there anyone special in your life? A boyfriend?"

Mallory's smile faded, and she looked away. "No. Not for quite some time."

Noticing that Mallory was wringing her hands, Max intently watched the interplay between Santa and his sister. "Just a minute, sweetie," he said to Cassidy as he strained to hear.

"I see." Santa paused, then gently probed some more. "So *that's* something you would like, isn't it?"

Her gaze snapped back to him. "I used to think so."

"But not now?" When Mallory merely shrugged, he continued, "Is that why you left college suddenly?"

Mallory stiffened. "My mom—"

"Yes, I know about your mom, and it was wonderful for you to be here while she went through her surgery and treatment," he said kindly. "But I hear she's doing really well now, and is back at work." He leaned closer to her, his blue eyes intent. "Yet here you are, still at home, not even taking a class or two online while you work at the eye clinic. It's as if, overnight, you've given up on all your dreams. What happened to your plans to live with your cousin Lettie while you worked on your master's degree? Or to come back after graduating to open your own architectural design firm?"

She drew back in alarm. "How could you possibly know that?" she asked, almost whispering.

Santa ignored her question and pressed on. "It's natural to want to put your life on hold, to take time to heal. But sometimes when we put our lives on hold, others close to us feel like they have to do the same." He paused as Mallory cast a sideways glance at her brother and then added, "So don't keep yourself closed off too long, Mallory. You may forget how to open up again… and keep your loved ones from realizing *their* dreams, too."

Anguished, she started to rise as she cried out in a low voice, "I don't know if I can!" Noticing Cassidy's puzzled look, she checked, cast a half-smile at her niece, and sank back down, gripping her

Karen Lail

hands tightly.

Santa patted her arm soothingly and waited a moment while she composed herself. "That's fear talking. Don't give in to it, Mallory— it will suck the spirit out of you. Even more, it will freeze your heart and paralyze your mind."

She looked at him, troubled. *Is my heart frozen?*

He searched her eyes earnestly. "Fear in small doses can protect you. But when you allow fear to dominate you, it keeps you from being who you were meant to be. You have to defeat it, Mallory. And the only way to defeat fear is to turn around, dig in your heels, and stare it down with the assurance that you are not alone. *That's* how you overcome it. *That's* how you move on." He cocked his head at her. "There was a song a group of brothers sang about 10 years ago… something about the Key of G? Do you remember it?"

Bewildered by the change in subject, she stared at him as teenage memories rushed through her. "The Locke Brothers," she murmured, "Christmas in the Key of G."

Santa nodded. "That's right: Christmas in the Key of G. Think about the lyrics, Mallory. Maybe it's time you start living that way again."

The photographer-elf chose that moment to take Mallory and Santa's picture.

"You look shell-shocked," Max observed several hours later, tossing the picture of Mallory and Santa onto the sparkling white quartz countertop of the kitchen island. Although the Glencoes lived in a century-old New England-style home, they had renovated and expanded the house the summer before Max and Mallory's sopho-more year of high school to make it more suitable for 21st-century living. That renovation had sparked Mallory's interest in architectural design and historic preservation. In fact, it had been Mallory who had chosen the colors for the exterior of the home: dark gray siding and crisp white trim—"Like a pilgrim," she'd said at the time—accented by a front door painted in her mother's favorite robin's egg blue.

Meredythe finished pouring tea into a seasonal red-and-white mug and handed it to her son before setting the coordinating teapot back on the trivet.

"Thanks, Mom." He blew gently on the hot tea and looked at his sister over the brim of the mug. "What exactly did he say to you?"

"It was uncanny, Max—it was like he knew everything that's happened in the past couple of years. He knew I left college suddenly to come home; that I'm working at the practice… He even knew about my plans to live with Lettie."

Roger set his mug on the countertop and leaned forward. "But, Mallory, Charles Guthrie has been playing Santa Claus since you and Max were in elementary school."

At that moment, Max's phone vibrated. Mallory caught a glimpse of a girl's picture and the name Harper lighting the screen before Max scooped up the phone from the countertop.

"It *wasn't* Mr. Guthrie," Max replied, hitting the Ignore button and setting the phone back down. "I don't think I've ever seen this Santa before."

"Maybe it was someone who recognized you from years ago—perhaps a teacher from high school, or someone in church?" Meredythe suggested as she nudged her mug to one side and rested her chin on her clasped hands.

Mallory considered it a moment, then shook her head. "No. No, I don't think so."

Roger stood up and carried his and Meredythe's empty mugs over to the sink. "Well, it's a small town, and people like to talk," he stated. "This Santa may have heard bits and pieces from different folks and stitched together a quilt, as the saying goes."

"I suppose so." She noticed Meredythe stroking the center of her forehead, her eyes closed. *She's been fading ever since Aidan and Phoebe picked up Cassidy.* "Why don't you go to bed, Mom? I'll clean up."

Meredythe slid from her stool. "Well, I was *hoping* to make it to ten o'clock tonight, but I don't think I can. It's been a tiring week."

"It was your first week working full-time again, so it's no wonder you're tired. But you'll get your stamina back in no time," Roger said bracingly, putting his hands on her shoulders and guiding her out of the kitchen. "Goodnight, kids."

"'Night," they answered, almost in unison.

Max picked up his vibrating phone again while Mallory took a sip of tea. Again Mallory saw Harper's name and picture before Max placed the phone face down. "Speaking of small towns: it looks like the word is out that I'm home from my trip," he said lightly. "Well, I guess I'll turn in, too—unless you need my help cleaning up?"

Mallory, however, was following her own train of thought. "Max, am I holding you back from anything?"

"What? *No!* What put *that* in your head?"

She concentrated on picking up the tea pot. "Something Santa said to me."

He pushed back his stool and sprang up almost angrily. "Look, just forget about the things he said to you, all right? What does *he* know?" he tossed over his shoulder as he stalked from the room.

Mallory's shock at her brother's outburst gave way to a mixture of sadness and regret. "I think he knows more than I realized," she murmured, cradling the warm tea pot against the suddenly cold pit in her stomach.

Los Angeles

The black Lincoln Navigator stretch limousine eased to the curb and stopped. On either side of the cordoned walkway, spectators, reporters, and paparazzi stirred, eyes and cameras focused on the chauffeur as he walked around the vehicle. After a moment, the chauffeur opened the passenger door and Graham stepped out, turned, and helped a very pregnant Shannon out of the car. Shannon took Graham's arm and smiled as Graham waved to the crowd. He and Shannon moved along the walkway towards the building while, behind them, Gabriel and Courtney exited the limo. They, too, paused while Gabriel waved, and then they trailed after Graham and Shannon. Next, Gareth and Rachel emerged, followed by Gideon and Rachel's twenty-five-year-old sister, Meghan. The four of them stood in a tight semicircle.

The crowd broke into speculative murmurs when they saw Gideon's date.

"Where's Trish?" a female reporter, whom Gideon had never seen before, asked, thrusting a microphone at him.

"Trish wasn't able to come tonight, so Rachel's sister Meghan very kindly agreed to join me," he replied, smiling down at Meghan. Then, with a nod and a wave to the crowd, he ushered Meghan forward, Gareth and Rachel falling in behind them.

The reporter looked after them curiously. All her instincts told her there was more to this story about Trish—she was sure of it.

Perhaps a call to Trish's agent would shed some light. That would have to wait until tomorrow, though.

She turned back to the street as the next limo pulled up to the curb.

CHAPTER 3

Saturday, December 15th
Hepton Grove

The clock at the bottom of the stairs was striking 9:00 a.m. when Mallory knocked on Max's bedroom door. After a moment, the door opened, and Max, still clad in the plaid lounge pants and T-shirt that served as his pajamas, leaned sleepily against the doorframe.

"I'm sorry—I didn't mean to wake you," Mallory said apologetically. "Go back to bed." She started to turn away, but Max laid a restraining hand on her arm.

"No, I'm glad you got me up." He rubbed the back of his neck with his other hand. "Look, Mal, I'm sorry I blew up at you last night."

At the mention of last night, Mallory's mind raced through Santa's words, leaving her awash in anguish again: *Given up on all your dreams... That's fear talking... Think about the lyrics.*

"Forgive me?" Max asked, squeezing her arm gently.

Mallory jolted back to the moment. "Of course. Don't worry about it. I know you were jetlagged from your trip."

"That's no excuse. I shouldn't have taken it out on you."

She wagged her finger at him with mock severity. "I'll forgive you this time, but if you do it again, I'm telling Mom!"

Max grinned as he grabbed her hand and shook it. "Deal." He scanned her head to toe, taking in her pearl-gray sweater, dark-wash skinny jeans, and boots. "Where are you off to?"

"Boy, you *are* jetlagged. Remember? The church Christmas party is tonight. I'm going to pick up the cupcakes and some snacks. I was also going to run by The Toy Trunk and get another toy or two for the toy drive. Do you need anything while I'm out?"

"No, thanks, I'm good. Hey, wait a minute." He grabbed his wallet off his dresser and pulled out two $20 bills. "Pick up an extra toy to donate."

She took the money from him with a smile. "All right."

"Will you be home in time to watch the football game?"

"If we get enough people to help decorate the fellowship hall." She shook her head. "I know it's been going on for years, but it still feels strange to watch an NFL game on Saturdays in December."

"I know. Well, I'll tell you what: I'll meet you at the church around noon so we can knock out the decorations and get home before the game. I want to see your face when the Rams lose and *I* win the bet."

"Sorry to burst your bubble, but the Rams are going to *win*, and no amount of decorating you do is going to get you out of paying up," she said, patting his shoulder before turning and heading down the stairs.

At a little after seven that evening, Mallory, Max, and their parents arrived at the church and stepped out of Roger's SUV.

Roger looked back at his son as they walked around the vehicle to join the women. "Well, I'm sorry you lost the bet, Max, but thank you for including us in the pay-off. Dinner was delicious." He stopped and leaned in close. "But I have to say, I would have picked the Rams, too," he said, clapping him on the shoulder before moving past him to grasp Meredythe's hand.

Max smiled sheepishly as Mallory handed him a toy and patted his shoulder, too, before following her parents.

Carrying their toy donations, they crossed the plowed church parking lot and entered the family life center. James and Emily Wyatt greeted the Glencoe family, James shaking hands warmly with Roger while Emily wrapped Meredythe in a fierce hug. "We'll catch up later," Emily promised Meredythe before she and James moved away to welcome the next arrivals.

Minutes later, their coats and scarves hung in the cloakroom, the family carefully deposited their toys in a bin marked "Hepton Grove Annual Toy Drive" before entering the large fellowship hall. The four of them stood there for a moment, a study in contrasts: Meredythe garbed in a cherry-red dress, and Roger and Max both sporting bright colored shirts and festive ties, but Mallory dressed more soberly in a black turtleneck sweater, a forest-green skirt, and black tights and boots.

Seeing his sister scanning the crowd anxiously, Max leaned to her and murmured, "Don't worry, they're not here."

Aidan and Phoebe approached, each holding one of Cassidy's hands. Cassidy broke loose from her parents and twirled around, showing off her red, green, and gold plaid taffeta dress.

"You look beautiful, Cassidy," Mallory said. "And I love those red shoes!"

"What do you say to Aunt Mallory?" Phoebe prompted.

"Thank you!" She held up a small wrapped candy cane. "I won a candy cane for *almost* pinning the red nose on Rudolph!"

"That is *awesome!*" Max enthused, giving her a high five.

At that moment, Pastor Daniel Cranford—a short, trim man in his mid-forties and known affectionately as "Pastor Dan"—blew a whistle and stepped forward into the middle of the room. "All right, everyone, it's time for the Three-Legged Present Dash. This round is for anyone aged eighteen and up, so grab your partner!"

"Come on, sis—let's show them how it's done!" Max said, pulling her over to claim one of the lanes that had been taped off on the floor.

"I'll help you get ready," Aidan offered, grabbing a long strip of red cloth from a basket. Minutes later, Mallory and Max stood side-by-side, her right leg bound to his left from ankle to calf. Aidan finished piling a chin-high stack of gift-wrapped boxes in Mallory's arms while Max waited patiently, bearing his own load of presents.

When each team was ready, Pastor Dan called, "On your mark! Get set!" and then blew his whistle. Staying within their respective lanes, the teams began loping toward the far end of the fellowship hall, where they had to turn and race back to their starting point. On either side of them, some competitors stumbled and others dropped their presents, but although Mallory's stack of boxes shifted precariously, she and Max managed to stay perfectly in step and cross the finish line without losing a single box. As winners, they had the privilege of handing out small candy canes to each of the other teams before receiving their own prize of regular-size candy canes.

"Twin power!" Max cried, touching his candy cane to Mallory's victoriously before stuffing it crook-side down in his shirt pocket.

And so the games went on: Santa's Sack Race, Reindeer Bowling, the Snowball-on-a-Spoon Race, and Snow-Hole. For those who preferred not to play, or simply wanted to take a break from the games, there were several stations on the opposite side of the fellowship hall where they could make felt Christmas ornaments, birch log candle holders, and other crafts, or enjoy snacks and drinks. Mallory and Max made all the rounds, laughing and chatting with their fellow contestants and crafts-mates. Seeing their children's obvious enjoyment, Roger and Meredythe exchanged a poignant smile.

It was just before eight-thirty. Max and Mallory were playing a game of Snow-Hole, and Mallory was just about to toss her last bean bag when she heard the sound of jingle bells. She, along with everyone else in the fellowship hall, stopped in mid-action and listened with eager anticipation as the jingling grew louder and louder. At last the door burst open and Santa came in, calling his familiar "Ho-ho-ho!"

Mallory's smile froze and instinctively she looked at Max, who was equally surprised. *This can't be happening!*

But it was: The Santa they had seen last night at Prescott's Department Store now stood there beaming as he surveyed the eager crowd of children pressing in around him.

Dreading a repeat of last night's encounter, Mallory looked around, panic-stricken, for a place to hide. Her eyes landed on a directional sign affixed over a doorway. *Of course! The sanctuary!* She turned slowly and then began walking, seemingly casually, towards the door.

From behind her, Santa's voice called out, "Mallory, since my elf has the night off, would you help me pass out the children's gifts?"

She halted in mid-step, eyes fixed longingly on her escape route. *Run!* her mind screamed at her, but her feet wouldn't cooperate. She was trapped. Resolutely she straightened her shoulders and turned around.

Faces were aimed at her. Some were curious. Some, like Cassidy's, showed excitement; others, like her parents', Max's, and even Pastor Dan's, registered surprise mixed with encouragement.

The suspended moment of silence stretched for several seconds. Meredythe laid a hand on Roger's arm in growing alarm, and then sighed as their daughter finally said, "Sure."

Santa beamed and beckoned her to join him and Pastor Dan.

Max moved behind Roger and Meredythe as Mallory advanced towards Santa. "That's the same Santa we saw at Prescott's last night," Max murmured.

"Ah," Roger replied. He leaned over to James Wyatt. "Where's Charles Guthrie?"

"Oh, didn't you hear? Their new granddaughter arrived ten weeks early and will be in the neonatal unit for about a month. He and Sylvia have gone to Georgia to help out with the kids so that their son and daughter-in-law can be with the baby as much as possible. We were lucky to find this Santa on such short notice." He glanced lovingly at his wife. "Emily calls it a miracle. This Santa had just finished a job in California a few days ago and as a favor to Charles, arranged to come east to fill in at Prescott's. Charles also asked him to stand in for him at our party, and he agreed to that too. So maybe it really was a miracle," he said, winking at Emily.

Roger nodded, eyeing Santa pensively.

Pastor Dan handed Santa a cinch-neck red velvet bag of gifts before escorting him to a seat of honor near the artificial Christmas tree that was nestled in a corner. The children—about twenty in all—gathered in a semicircle on the floor in front of Santa, Cassidy at his right side. At Pastor Dan's direction, Mallory stood to Santa's left, between Santa and Pastor Dan.

"Now, kids, I know you're very excited about Santa being here," Pastor Dan said with a smile and nod to Santa. "But keep in mind that while Christmas is a time when we give and receive gifts to and from our family and friends—and from Santa, of course—the Bible says that every *good and perfect* gift comes from God in heaven. Toys may break, bikes may rust, and clothes may be outgrown, but God's love for each of you is a gift that can never wear out. And as proof of that love, He sent His Son, Jesus, the most Perfect Gift of all. Santa only comes for a season, but God the Father, Son, and Holy Spirit is with you every day of the year. So, as you come forward for your gift from your church family, think about how much God loves you and wants you to love Him too." Pastor Dan stretched out a hand towards Santa. "Santa?"

"Thank you, Pastor Dan. That was beautifully said." Santa beckoned to Mallory, and she leaned down as he pulled open the bag. "You know all of the children here, don't you?"

She scanned the semicircle of excited kids and mentally recited their names. *Zack, Cooper, Caden, Henleigh, Penelope, Liam, Lily...* "Yes, I sure do."

"Good. Now, if you would bring a child up to me and introduce them, I'll spend a minute or two talking to them and give them their present, and then we'll do it all over again for the next child, and so on, okay?"

"Okay."

Santa drew out the first present and Mallory bent down to the sandy-haired little boy sitting in front of her. "Zack, you're first," she said with a smile.

Grinning, he took Mallory's outstretched hand and scrambled to his feet.

Santa and Zack exchanged a few murmured words and then "Merry Christmas, Zack," Santa said, handing him the small wrapped box and beaming when Zack thanked him.

"This is Cooper," Mallory announced, shepherding the next little boy over to Santa's lap as Zack scampered away. Once Cooper was nestled against Santa's broad chest, Mallory walked to the next child and, holding his hand, waited until Santa held out a present to Cooper.

"Thanks, Santa," Cooper said as he took the present and slid from Santa's lap.

Mallory continued bringing the children forward one by one to receive their gifts, ending with Cassidy, who hugged Santa impulsively before skipping off to her parents.

Santa cinched the bag closed, stood up, and placed the bag on his chair as he faced Mallory. He reached out and took her hand gently. "Thank you for your help—you were a great elf!"

"It was my pleasure." And, with a start, she realized she wasn't mouthing a platitude to be polite—she had truly enjoyed helping.

He released her hand and, before she could move away, raised a detaining finger. "Oh! And," he said, reaching into one of his capacious coat pockets, "I always give my elves a little thank you gift to show my appreciation." He pressed a flat, wrapped gift into her hand. "So thank you again, Mallory. I hope you'll give some more thought to what we talked about last night."

She gave a hesitant nod.

He beamed at her. "Good." He let go of Mallory's hand and turned as Pastor Dan and his wife, Linda, approached.

"Thank you so much for coming on such short notice. Santa's visit is always the highlight of the party for the children," the pastor said, gripping Santa's hand.

"I was glad to do it."

"You're more than welcome to stay and have some snacks."

"I appreciate that, but I think I'll just head back to the hotel."

"Well, here are some cookies to take with you," Linda Cranford said, handing him a sandwich-size storage bag. "We all know how Santa loves cookies."

"Yes, I do," he replied with a laugh as he tucked the bag into a pocket. "Thank you."

"Our pleasure," said Pastor Dan. "Now if you'll excuse us, I promised my wife I would serve the punch."

"Of course." He cast a glance at Mallory. "Goodbye, Mallory. Have a Merry Christmas. You, too, Max," he said as Max joined his sister.

"Merry Christmas," they chorused in reply.

"And thank you for the gift!" Mallory added. Her eyes tracked him as Santa walked to the center of the room. With a wave, Santa called "Merry Christmas to all, and to all a good night!" Mallory found herself waving back at him.

"So what did he give you, Sis?"

Mallory gently tore away the wrapping paper. "Luggage tags."

How odd, she thought, fingering the brightly colored tags and watching Santa head out the door amid cries of farewell.

───────────────

Carrying the luggage tags in one hand and her purse in the other, Mallory entered her bedroom and nudged the door partially closed with an elbow. At twelve feet by ten feet, hers was the smallest of the four bedrooms, but she hadn't minded the size. From the moment she'd first toured the house as a five-year-old child, she'd known this was the room she wanted. It could have been half its size and she still would have chosen it because it was the only bedroom with a window seat.

Nestled between two deep closets on the long outer wall, the window seat was the stuff of fairy dust and enchanted dreams. During the princess and pirate days of her childhood years, it served variously as the turret of a castle, the crow's nest of a ship, or Cinderella's pumpkin coach. In her tween years after seeing a movie version of Aladdin, Mallory had requested to change the lavender and mint green sprigged curtains and pillows for a tent-like enclosure of filmy white voile. Using the sewing skills she had learned from the pastor's wife that summer, she had made tasseled bolsters and pillows to line the window seat. Lounging in the "tent," she and Lettie would sit and share secrets, experiment with new hairstyles, or obsess over the latest teen heartthrob.

When the Glencoes had undertaken the renovation of their house eleven years ago, their architect had recommended removing the window seat and double-hung window to create a space for a built-in desk and shelves with a small transom window near the ceiling. Mallory was appalled. How could she explain to the architect that this was her retreat, her place to read, to ponder, to weave plans and dream dreams? In the end, she acknowledged that the built-in would free up some floor space, but argued that the window seat was part of the charm of the room. The architect conceded; the plans were revised and the window seat was preserved, the woodwork painted a soft shade of ash gray, a cushion upholstered in a sophisticated

Karen Lail

jewel-toned paisley with teal piping substituted for the bolsters, and the tent-like structure replaced by a Roman shade of the same paisley fabric—furnishings that had carried her through to the present day.

It was to the window seat that she now retreated, her face troubled.

I hope you'll give some more thought to what we talked about last night.

She shook her head in vexation as she placed her purse and the luggage tags beside her on the cushion. She had thought of little else in her free moments since last night's encounter at Prescott's. Well, that wasn't exactly true: she had focused more on her *feelings*—the shock and sadness and humiliation—not what she and Santa had actually *said*. Now, leaning her head against the embrasure, she went back over their conversation point by point until her mind zeroed in on one of the last things Santa had spoken last night.

"'Think about the lyrics,'" she echoed, raising her head, her eyes searching out the box labeled CDs on one of the floating shelves above the narrow console table that served as her desk. Springing up, she crossed the room, lifted down the box and set aside the lid, and then riffled through the cases. Removing one of the cases, she held it against her like a forgotten treasure as she returned to her spot on the window seat.

She rested the case on her lap, her fingers drifting across the cover title... "The Locke Brothers: Christmas in the Key of G." Smiling wistfully, she leaned back and yielded to the tugging of her teenaged memories.

November, ten years ago. The Madison Square Garden marquee read "The Locke Brothers Christmas Tour." Meredythe and Kaye Glencoe had brought their 16-year-old daughters to New York City for a long weekend as an early Christmas present, and the concert was the highlight of the trip. Mallory and Lettie had laughed as their moms had inserted those little foam earplugs in their ears, but soon wished they had their own pairs, for, when the announcer had said, "Here they are for their Christmas concert: Gabriel, Graham, Gideon, and Gareth—the Locke Brothers," a tsunami of female screams crashed through the arena as the boys ran onstage and took their places with their instruments. The boys led off with "Joy to the World" followed by a rock rendition of "Angels We Have Heard on High." And then, towards the middle of the program, Gabriel had said: "Now here's Gideon singing a song he and I wrote, called 'Christmas in the Key of G'. We hope you like it."

Pulling herself back to the present, Mallory opened the case, slipped the booklet from the left side, and located the page with the title song's lyrics. She scanned the page until her gaze landed on one of the verses:

> Sharing the gift of Christmas,
> Living my faith for all to see,
> To gladden hearts that once had no hope,
> No matter the cost to me.

Living my faith for all to see... no matter the cost to me.
"Maybe it's time to start living that way again," Santa had said. Mallory sighed as she reinserted the booklet, closed the CD case, and laid it next to the luggage tags on the window seat. He'd made it sound so simple, like she could just flip a switch or snap her fingers and magically be the same girl she'd been eighteen months ago. Sometimes, like tonight at the church party, she would get caught up in the fun of the moment and cherish the hope that she really could put everything behind her. But then other times, like last night at Prescott's when Santa had seemed to peer into her soul, she felt raw... exposed... *frozen.*

In her mind, she could hear Santa's words again: "It will freeze your heart and paralyze your mind."

She buried her face in her hands. *Oh, God, please make this vicious*

Karen Lail

cycle stop!

Her head jerked up when a tap sounded and her bedroom door creaked open.

"I didn't mean to startle you," Meredythe said softly, pulling her floral satin robe tightly around her thin body as she crossed the room. It still hurt Mallory to see how frail her mom looked.

"It's okay," she answered, tossing her purse onto her bed and shifting over to make room for her mom. "I thought you were asleep."

Meredythe settled her robe about her as she sat down. "I couldn't turn my mind off tonight."

"Is something wrong?"

She reached out and grasped Mallory's hands. "Oh, I've been thinking about you, and me, and these past eighteen months or so... How proud I am of you, and how sorry—so *very* sorry, Mallory—that I haven't been more present for you."

Mallory pulled her hands away only to wrap her arms tightly around her mother. "Mom... *no!* You have *nothing* to apologize for." She drew back to look at her. "You were fighting *cancer!* I was—"

"You were going through something just as devastating, and I was too worn down by my own battle to be able to help you. And your Dad was so torn—he wanted to be there for you, too, but I kept him so busy running back and forth for treatments, then nursing me through the side effects, all while he was trying to keep up with the practice..." She smiled tremulously. "I was *so* relieved when Max offered to move back home. I knew he at least would be able to focus on you."

A pang pierced her, and Mallory looked away sadly, hugging herself. *So Santa was right: Max really did put his life on hold because of me.*

"I'm sorry—I didn't mean to dredge it all up again." Meredythe continued. "I just wanted to say how well I thought you handled everything tonight. I know seeing Santa again was a shock, especially after everything he said to you last night, but you saw it through, and I was so proud of you."

Mallory fingered the CD cover beside her and then looked at her mother. "I have to say, I had a good time helping with the kids. The whole night was fun. And, to be honest, it was telling, Mom. Last night I was too stunned and overwhelmed to think about what Santa said. But seeing him again tonight… well, I've been trying to move past some of the shock and really think about his words."

"I'm glad to hear that. If there's one thing this bout with cancer has taught me, it's that life is too short and too precious to be wasted in fear."

There's that word again… fear. "So what are you saying, Mom?"

"What I'm saying is that this is *not* the life you're supposed to be living, Mallory. Don't get me wrong—we love having you at home and working with us at the clinic, but we *know* this is not what you wanted. You wanted to live with Lettie while you got your master's degree. You wanted to hang up your shingle as an architectural designer."

"Yeah, but the plan was to go to graduate school in Albany, less than two hours away. She's moved clear across the country. I don't want to live out there. I'm a New England girl."

"I'm not saying you should *move* to California… just go for a visit. You know Lettie has been begging you to fly out. She's homesick for you, Mallory—you two have been more like sisters than cousins." Meredythe pulled an envelope labeled Westcott Travel from her pocket and held it out to Mallory. "So go have a change of scenery, just like Max did. It will do you good to get away. And when you come back, well, maybe you'll be ready to decide what you want to do next."

Tentatively, Mallory took the envelope, lifted the flap, and removed and unfolded the travel itinerary. "Oh, my gosh, Mom. First class?"

"It's a long trip to spend cramped in economy. Consider it a Christmas bonus from your dad and me for all your work at the clinic. We really want you to take this time to enjoy yourself… to celebrate how far you've come and look ahead to whatever is on the horizon."

Struggling with the familiar feeling of panic, she forced her lips into a smile. "I don't know what to say. Thank you," she said, hugging her mom again.

"You're welcome." Meredythe drew back and looked encouragingly at her daughter. "Look, you're ready for this, Mallory. And, trust me, once you're in Los Angeles with Lettie, the time will fly by."

"Does she know I'm coming?"

"No, I told your Aunt Kaye about it, but we agreed Lettie would want to hear it from you." She laid her hand against Mallory's cheek briefly before rising. "Goodnight, sweetheart."

"'Night, Mom." As the door softly closed, Mallory studied the itinerary more closely. Yes, there was the statement she'd dreaded: All Tickets Are Non-Refundable. The page and the envelope fluttered to the floor in front of her as she dropped her head into her hands. There was no getting out of it. And no matter what her mom said, she wasn't sure she was ready for this trip. Oh, once she got to L.A., it would be all right. Lettie would be there. But flying out there and back, *alone*...

The promise from Hebrews 13:5 filled her: "God has said, 'Never will I leave you. Never will I forsake you.'"

She exhaled gently and lowered her hands. *Thank you, God.*

Absently picking up one of the luggage tags and twirling the strap around her index finger, she raised her head and looked at the wall calendar above her desk. December 15. Just six more days until the clinic closed for the Christmas holiday.

From the time she was fourteen, Mallory had been helping out at the practice in one capacity or another, and she had been working full-time since October when the receptionist went out on maternity leave. But the receptionist would be returning to work the Monday after New Year's Day. Max would be heading back to college to resume his graduate studies. *And ready, or not, I guess I'm going to California.*

And then she froze, staring at the tag. Had Santa somehow *known* her parents were going to send her on this trip?

No, surely his choice of a gift was just a coincidence.

Wasn't it?

It had to be—just a nice, safe gift that one stranger could give to another without raising eyebrows.

Setting the tag aside, she stretched forward to remove her phone from her purse, and leaned back as the screen lit up. She started to press the FaceTime icon but thought better of it. Lettie and her family were visiting Lettie's maternal grandmother in Florida. There was no telling who might be around to overhear. Plus, Lettie had an uncanny ability to know when she was trying to hide something—she wasn't ready to share all of what had been happening the past two days.

No, a text message was safer.

> *Mallory:* Hope you're enjoying Florida! I'll miss seeing you this Christmas.

A few seconds later, Lettie answered:

> *Lettie:* I miss you too! But Florida is great! What are you up to?

Mallory paused for a moment and then smiled as her eyes lighted on the CD cover.

> *Mallory:* Doing some reminiscing. Can you believe it's been over TEN YEARS since our trip to NYC to see the Locke Brothers?

> *Lettie:* OMG! Best Christmas present EVER! What made you think of that???

> *Mallory:* It's a long story.

> *Lettie:* So…?

Mallory hesitated, looking again at the CD for a long moment before finally replying.

> *Mallory:* So… I'll tell you about it when I come to L.A. for a visit, if your offer still stands.

Karen Lail

And then Lettie's reply popped up, led by hearts and smiley faces:

Lettie: YES!!! When???

Mallory reached down for the itinerary and looked at the trip dates. Two weeks.

Mallory: Tuesday, January 8th, to Tuesday, January 22nd.

Lettie answered:

Lettie: Just tell me what time you'll get in to LAX and I'll meet you! There's so much I want to show you and tell you!

And then a follow-up remark:

Lettie: UPDATE: THIS will be the best Christmas present ever! I can't believe it!!!!

CHAPTER 4

Sunday, December 16th

Los Angeles

"I can't believe it!" Gideon closed the tabloid and re-read the cover headline with a look of shock mingled with disgust:

> Trish 'Un-Lockes' from Gideon, Cries "He's just
> a player!"

Gabriel pulled the tabloid from Gideon's grasp. "No wonder she begged you not to hate her. What a tissue of lies," he said with a curl of his lip as he tossed the paper into the kitchen recycle bin.

"She only did it to try to get publicity for her acting career," Graham reasoned.

"Come on, Graham, don't make excuses for her. She didn't have to go this far," Gideon retorted.

"What are you going to do?" Gabriel asked.

"What *can* I do? If I ignore it, the press will say there's something to her story. If I deny it, they'll go on a 'He Said/She Said' feeding frenzy."

"You could show them the texts that she sent when she broke up with you."

"Yeah, and then they'll either say I'm a cad for showing the messages, or that I somehow faked them." He spun around in frustration. "I'm *sick* of this life!"

Gabriel and Graham exchanged a concerned look. They'd been hearing comments like this more and more frequently from Gideon in recent weeks.

Gabriel cast a glance towards the family room, where Gareth and Rachel cuddled together on the sofa while they watched the end of "It's a Wonderful Life."

"Well, when Gareth and Rachel announce their engagement in a couple of weeks, the press will have something different to feed on," he said quietly.

"Don't count on it," Gideon scoffed. "You watch: they'll find a way to dredge it all up again. I just hope this doesn't make Rachel hesitate about accepting Gareth's proposal."

"Surely not," Gabriel protested.

"Has Kendra said anything?" Graham asked. Kendra Thomas had been their publicist since the brothers first hit the teen music scene.

"I haven't heard from her." At that moment, Gideon's phone rang. He pulled it out of his back pocket and looked at the caller ID. "Oh, here she is now." He answered the phone. "Hello, Kendra... Yes, Gabriel got it and showed it to me... No, I had no idea... No, she sent me a text and said we should just end it... Yes, *a text*... No, I never cheated on her. All I did was take Rachel's sister to a party in Trish's place, and that was *after* she broke up with me... Who?... No, please don't do that. I just want to ignore it as much as possible." He sighed heavily. "Look, no matter what happens, the press is going to have a field day with this. I think it's better to just do nothing—especially with Graham and Shannon getting ready to have their baby, and..." he lowered his voice, "... Gareth's news that will be breaking soon. I don't want anything to taint that." He listened for a moment. "All right, but I want to see it first, okay? All right. Thanks, Kendra. You're the best!"

"Does she have a plan?" Graham asked.

"She wanted me to give an interview to some entertainment correspondent named Caitlyn Snow. I've never heard of her."

"Oh, I have—she just joined the staff of that celebrity news show that airs on weekday evenings," Gabriel said.

"Well, I told Kendra I didn't want to do it. She said I'd be making a mistake if I just kept quiet, so she's going to draft a press release for me to look at instead."

"Press release? What for?" Gareth asked as he and Rachel walked hand-in-hand into the kitchen.

His three brothers exchanged a look. At last, Gideon shrugged his shoulders. "He needs to know."

Gabriel pulled the tabloid from the recycle bin and slid it across the kitchen island. Gareth reached out and turned it so he and Rachel could see the cover. His eyes flew to Gideon. "Oh, man, I can't believe she did this to you."

He started to open the tabloid, but Gabriel forestalled him by placing his hand firmly on the paper. "Don't bother—the headline says it all," he said, tugging the paper away from Gareth and dropping it disgustedly back in the recycle bin.

Their father, Garrison, strode into the kitchen, his cell phone pressed to his ear. "Understood. Thanks for calling. We'll talk later." He ended the call and looked at each of his sons. "We need to have a family meeting. Can we do it now?"

Translated, that meant: "We're doing it *now*."

Gideon closed his eyes. *Great.*

"I guess I'd better go," Rachel said, leaning forward to brush her lips against Gareth's.

"I'm sorry to interrupt your plans," Garrison told her.

"It's all right. The movie was over anyway," she answered.

"I'll call you later," Gareth promised. Rachel nodded, laying a sympathetic hand on Gideon's arm before walking out of the kitchen.

"Give me a second while I text Courtney," Gabriel said to Garrison, pulling out his phone.

Graham's thumbs were busily typing on his own device. "And I'm texting Shannon."

"That's fine," Garrison answered. "Meet us in the family room when you're ready. Come on, Gareth. Gideon."

Gareth stood outside the pool house-turned-rehearsal studio located in the far right corner of the fenced-in backyard. Gideon had disappeared without a word as soon as the family meeting had adjourned almost two hours ago. Gareth had suspected he'd retreated here, but as the dinner hour approached with no sign of him, Gareth decided to come out and check on his brother.

Listening closely, he could hear Gideon working to the climax of the drum solo that always marked the midpoint of their performance when the brothers were on tour. He could picture the concentration on Gideon's face as he silently, perfectly kept time, the drumsticks a blur as he moved effortlessly between the snares, the toms, and the cymbals, his right foot frenziedly working the pedal of the bass drum while the left tapped the pedal of the hi-hat. With a final clash of a cymbal, the solo ended, and Gareth pushed open the door.

Gideon sat behind his drum kit, shoulders sagging and head bowed, sweat dripping from his hair. Gareth walked over to the small beverage fridge, pulled out a bottle of water, and handed it to Gideon.

"Thanks," Gideon said hoarsely, twisting off the cap and drinking deeply.

The extra snare drum tucked in the corner caught and held Gareth's gaze. He had a sudden flashback to a time nearly twelve years ago when Gideon had patiently taught him to play snare well enough for the two of them to perform a "dueling drums" piece. The look of pride on Gideon's face had matched his own when they had debuted the number for the family. Gideon had lobbied to include it in that year's tour, but Gabriel and Graham—who were engaged in some sort of teenage feud with Gideon at the time—had been opposed to it, and Dad had agreed that Gideon's solo was enough. Gideon had offered to drop his solo so they could perform together, but Dad had vetoed that, too. The boys all had their assigned instruments: Gabriel played lead guitar, Graham was on keyboards, Gideon was the drummer, and Gareth was the bass player. Their backup band was paid to augment those instruments as needed, so it was frivolous to have Gareth play drums too. Period, end of story.

Yet Gideon and Gareth had continued to practice the piece off and on in the ensuing years, particularly after their brothers had married and moved out of the house; less frequently since their mom had died.

On impulse, Gareth now pulled the snare drum out of the corner, placed it opposite Gideon's drum kit, and removed the cover. "I'm a little rusty, but how about playing the duel?"

Karen Lail

Gideon smiled wearily and, one at a time, tossed over two of the four extra drumsticks he always kept beside him when he played. Taking one more swig of water, he replaced the cap, set down the bottle, and wiped his forehead with the back of his hand.

Drumsticks poised upright like two duelers saluting with their swords, he and Gareth stared with mock ferocity at each other and then, breaking into a wicked grin, Gideon led off with the opening attack…

Later, clad in a fresh pair of jeans and blotting his damp hair with a towel, Gideon emerged amidst a cloud of steam from his side of the Jack-and-Jill bathroom he and Gareth shared and found Gareth stretched out on his bed.

"Did you lose your way to your room?" he teased, chucking the towel at his brother.

Gareth caught the towel and swung his legs off the bed as he sat up. "I've been waiting for you. I thought maybe you and I could go do something tonight. It's been a while since we've hung out together."

Gideon pulled on a gray Henley shirt. "I thought you and Rachel were going to watch another Christmas movie tonight."

Gareth shrugged. "We decided to postpone it until tomorrow."

Gideon studied his brother skeptically. "Gareth, I'm fine—you don't need to babysit me. Kendra has sent out the press release, and hopefully it will put an end to all this nonsense that Trish and her agent have stirred up."

"I know. But Rachel has already made plans to have a Christmas craft night with her mom instead."

"Oh, nice. You're smart to stay away—I've seen you with a glue gun," Gideon teased.

He gave an answering grin. "Hey, I've gotten better at it." His expression turned wistful. "We used to have a lot of fun doing that sort of thing when Mom was alive, didn't we?"

"Yeah, we sure did."

"Do you think Dad is ready yet?"

"Ready for what?"

"To do the whole Christmas thing. I mean, this is the first year we haven't been on the road somewhere over the holidays. I was just hoping that... you know... maybe he was ready to—"

"Forgive myself?" Garrison interjected from the open doorway where he had been standing, unseen, for the past minute or so. "The answer is, no, I will never forgive myself. But if you want to decorate the house for Christmas this year, we will."

"Well, maybe just a tree. We don't need to go all-out," Gareth said.

"All right, son... a tree it is."

It had been more of an ordeal than any of them had imagined.

Draping the tree with the white-beaded garland she had hand-strung during the long tedious hours traveling on a chartered bus during their first summer tour. Hanging each ornament their mother had made or had guided their own young hands to form. Carefully unwrapping and placing the treasured keepsakes from their mom and dad's first years of marriage.

But at last it was done, and, eyes moist with emotion, father and sons sat in semidarkness looking at the lighted tree, each cherishing his own memories of the woman who had been wrenched from them too soon.

CHAPTER 5

Tuesday, December 18th

Los Angeles

"It looks like the media have picked up your press release," Garrison observed, joining Gideon and Gareth at the kitchen island where they were eating plates of scrambled eggs, toast, and fruit. "And at least one network has gotten statements from Trish, too. This one aired last night," he said, passing his phone over. Gideon pressed the Play arrow for the video Garrison had cued up. A man and a woman stood side-by side in front of a large monitor that displayed the same tabloid headline Gideon had seen on Sunday. With alarm, Gideon realized the woman was the female reporter who had asked him about Trish the night of the label's Christmas party.

> *Bob:* "Caitlyn, I understand there's been a development on the Gideon Locke-Trish Galloway front."

> *Caitlyn:* "That's right, Bob. Gideon Locke has broken his silence on Trish Galloway's claim that he is 'just a player.' In a statement released over the weekend, Locke said, and I quote, 'Trish knows there hasn't been anyone else during the course of our relationship. There were two occasions when, because Trish was double-booked, I took a family friend to parties in Trish's place—Trish knew about it and was fine with it. And after Trish broke up with me, I took that same family friend to our record company's Christmas party. The truth is that Trish and I just have different priorities right now. I am looking to

settle down, but Trish wants to focus on her career. While I feel our careers and our relationship don't have to be mutually exclusive, Trish disagrees. Trish is quite an actress and I sincerely wish her every success.' End quote. Trish corroborated Locke's story, but attributed the cause of the break to professional jealousy. Here's what she had to say:"

Gideon leaned forward as Trish's face appeared on the monitor behind Caitlyn. Trish tossed her head and spoke into the microphone held out to her.

> *Trish:* "He couldn't accept that my career is starting to take off while his is—well, stagnant. He is looking for somebody—or perhaps I should say *a 'nobody'*—who is less successful than he is."

Gideon slumped back. *Oh, Trish, when did you get so nasty?*

> *Caitlyn:* "Kendra Thomas, publicist for The Locke Brothers, offered this comment, and I quote: 'To characterize Gideon's career as being stagnant is unfair and untrue. Gideon and his brothers are not making any appearances this holiday season for the simple reason that Graham and his wife Shannon are expecting their first child in January. Graham quite naturally wanted to stay close to home during this time, and the whole family is looking forward to welcoming Graham and Shannon's baby girl. The brothers are scheduled to perform in Branson for six weeks beginning in mid-April,

and will be starting another tour the third week of June."

Bob: "Very interesting, Caitlyn. I guess time will tell if fans of the Locke Brothers will stand behind Gideon… or show their allegiance to Trish by boycotting the performances."

Tight-lipped, Gideon exited the video and handed the phone back to his father. "Excuse me," he said, getting up and striding to the back door. The door closed behind him with a snap.

Gareth started after him, but Garrison grabbed his shoulder and pressed him gently but firmly back onto his stool. "Let *me* go, son. I know where to find him."

Garrison softly pushed open the door to the studio. Gideon sat motionless at the drum kit, forearms resting on his legs, his gaze focused on his clasped hands. Wordlessly, Garrison settled on the piano bench and waited.

At last, Gideon looked over at his father. "I always wondered what, if anything, would make me want to leave the entertainment business. I never dreamed it would be because of a girl breaking up with me."

"Gideon, *all* of you have talked about leaving show business at one time or another—granted, it was usually at the end of a tour, when everyone was overtired and short-tempered. But the point is, your mother and I said from the very beginning that any time you boys wanted to stop performing, it would be fine with us—as long as you fulfilled whatever commitments had already been lined up. That hasn't changed."

Gideon nodded mutely.

"So what's *really* bothering you, son? This isn't the first time the press has been hard on you."

He sighed. "It's this accusation that I'm 'a player.' On the one hand, it's made me so angry: Trish isn't just insulting *me*—she's attacking you and Mom, and how you raised us. But on the other… These past few months being with Trish, I've seen how easily show business can twist someone, maybe without their realizing it. So I've started questioning if it's changed me, too."

"Of course you've changed, but not in a bad way—your mom saw to that, God bless her. I'm proud of all of you—each of you has managed to stay grounded despite all the attention you've had over the years. And certainly no one can accuse you of living a lavish lifestyle since you still live at home with me," he said with a smile. "But you've had several very public relationships in the past couple of years so, right or wrong, Trish's claim that you're a player is easy for people to believe." He leaned forwarded earnestly. "To be honest Gideon, I think you've been trying *too* hard to find your soulmate. She's out there somewhere, and you *will* find her—you just need to be patient."

Gideon's mouth twisted wryly. "That's odd… a guy said almost the exact same thing to me just the other day."

"Smart man," Garrison remarked as he stood up. He placed a hand on Gideon's shoulder. "Now about you leaving the group… Don't make a snap decision. Wait until this situation with Trish has died down. If you still want to quit or even just scale back a little, well, we'll have a family meeting to talk about how to make that happen."

"Thanks, Dad," he replied gratefully, bumping his father's outstretched fist with his own.

Santa leaned close to Gideon and pointed off in the distance. "You'll have to go carefully, but there lies your happiness." Gideon strained to make out the features of the female form on the horizon. If only he could get a little closer…

The book slipped from his fingers, jarring him awake. Gideon peered sleepily at the wall clock in the living room. Almost ten-thirty. Closing and laying the book on the end table, he stood up, stretched, and then carried his stainless steel water bottle into the kitchen. As he reached for the refrigerator door, he glanced into the family room where Gareth and Rachel were curled up together watching "Miracle on 34th Street," Gareth's right arm stretched behind her along the sofa, her left hand held in his. As if he felt Gideon's gaze, Gareth cut his eyes to him and they shared a conspiratorial smile, each of them picturing the small dark blue ring box that sat upstairs on Gareth's dresser. Gareth cast a sidelong glance at Rachel before looking back at the TV, and Gideon turned his attention back to filling his bottle from the pitcher of filtered water.

Unsettled by his dream, Gideon stepped outside the kitchen door and wandered over to the pool deck. Impervious to the coolness of the evening, he searched the night sky, trying to see beyond the dull orange-yellow aura of the city lights, the breeze seeming to echo Santa and Garrison's words: "Be patient."

It was so hard to wait. Ever since Graham and Shannon's wedding three years ago, he'd desperately tried to find the same genuine, enduring, *reciprocated* love his parents and each of his brothers had been blessed with, but it had always eluded him.

And now that Trish had turned her back on their relationship, it seemed even farther away.

But maybe the right girl, whoever and wherever she may be, would come into his life soon.

"Please, God," he whispered.

There is no birth order to love, my son.

With sudden clarity, he realized that so many events in his life with his brothers *had* occurred in birth order—starting kindergarten, learning to drive, going on the first date—so it was only natural that when first Gabriel and then Graham had found their wives, Gideon assumed he would be the next one to marry. But when his youngest brother seemed to be falling in love, Gideon had redoubled his efforts to find his life's partner, trying to maintain that strict order... with the result that one relationship after another had fallen apart.

He'd been going about it all wrong, all along.

He took a deep breath. "All right, God. I'll take a step back and trust that it will happen in Your time."

CHAPTER 6

Tuesday, January 8th

Hepton Grove

The weather had not cooperated. In the days leading up to her departure, Mallory had checked the forecast frequently, secretly hoping a nor'easter or a lake-effect storm would hit, dumping several feet of snow on either Albany, where her trip would originate, or Philadelphia, where she would board the jumbo jet that would wing her cross-country.

But a quick check of her phone's weather app proved that no catastrophic storm had materialized. Although the temperatures across the region were in the low teens, the day of departure had dawned sunny and cloud-free in Philadelphia; in upstate New York, the snowplows had made short work of the meager two inches of snow that had fallen there overnight.

Her last hope melted away.

The logistics for getting Mallory to the airport had been complicated. Because Roger and Meredythe both had early-morning patients, and Max had returned to his college over the weekend, none of them was able to drive her. As of last week's prenatal appointment, Phoebe was prohibited from driving more than an hour at a time, so Mallory did not even ask her to make the four-hour round trip. In the end, Aidan, who had a 7:00 a.m. consultation at the hospital in Lake George, suggested that Mallory accompany him to the hospital and have an Uber driver meet them there.

It was just before 5:00 a.m. when Aidan picked up Mallory. Sensing his sister's disquiet, he maintained a steady stream of light-hearted chatter, winning a few laughs from her as they traveled east-southeast towards Lake George. As Aidan downshifted and turned into the main entrance of the hospital, Mallory impulsively rested her hand atop his on the gear shift. "Thank you, Aidan."

He cast a smile at her as he pulled to the curb and switched off the car. "You're going to be fine."

Just then, the Uber driver arrived. Aidan and the driver transferred her baggage to the black SUV. The driver closed the hatch and waited patiently as Mallory gave Aidan a quick hug and, face averted, stepped into the vehicle. The driver closed her door and walked around to the driver's side. Mallory wiped away a tear surreptitiously, then turned and waved brightly to Aidan as the SUV pulled away from the curb.

"Would you like to listen to the radio?" the driver asked.

"Sure."

"Is the Mickey and Sylvia morning show all right with you?"

"Yes, that's fine."

He tuned in the popular morning drive show.

But instead of listening to the humorous banter and periodic traffic reports, she reflected on the past couple of weeks. She hadn't realized it at the time, but there had been a kind of desperation in how she had tried to cram all of her family's holiday traditions into the space of a few days. The events of the Christmas holidays cycled through her mind like a series of vignettes. Baking and decorating a variety of cookies, and placing them in festive tins to give to family and friends. Caroling at the nursing home. Sewing stockings, filling them with some of the wish-list items for the shut-ins of their church, and delivering those gift-filled stockings: a box of Earl Grey tea bags and a tin of scones for Mrs. Winslow; bottles of Old Spice and English Leather cologne for Mr. Jenkins; Sudoku puzzle books, erasers, and .7 mm pencil lead refills for Mr. Rinaldi; skeins of brightly colored wool for Miss Kaminsky, who loved to crochet. And then attending the four o'clock Christmas Eve service and, once back home, watching a marathon of their favorite holiday movies. Opening the first present at midnight—always a set of pajamas—before heading to bed. Gathering around the tree Christmas morning to open the remaining gifts. Helping to prepare Christmas brunch and Christmas dinner. Playing

Monopoly as they waited to welcome in the New Year. And finally, two days ago, tackling the job of taking down the ornaments and decorations and packing them away until next year.

"Mallory, why don't you take down the stockings," her mom had suggested, "and then Max can take care of the garland."

"Okay," the twins agreed.

But as Mallory lifted her stocking from its hook under the mantel, she'd realized it was no longer empty. "That's odd."

"What's wrong?" Max had asked.

"There's something in here," she'd said, reaching into the stocking.

The box was squat and approximately three-and-a-half inches square. A gold-bordered name tag with her name written in Meredythe's flowing script adorned the front.

"Go ahead. Open it," her mother had urged.

She'd gently torn away the wrapping paper. Lifting the lid and the square layer of cotton, she'd found a rose gold bangle bracelet nestled inside.

"Oh, wow," was all she could say.

"It's from all of us: Mom, Aidan, Phoebe, Max, and me. Read the engraving," Roger had prompted.

Slowly rotating the bracelet, she'd softly read the words of two verses of scripture, separated by delicate filigree designs—verses that she had clung to for the past eighteen months.

The first was from Psalm 56:

"In God I trust and am not afraid."

The second was the words of Jesus from Mark 5:

"Don't be afraid; just believe."

"Wow," she repeated, slipping the bracelet on her left wrist.

"In other words," Max had said bracingly, "be bold. You can do this."

I hope so, she'd thought.

The ringing of her phone roused her from her abstraction. "Hi, Max," she said as the Uber driver turned down the radio.

"Hi, sis. I just wanted to check in with you before I head to class. Are you at the airport yet?"

Mallory's stomach churned and the saliva in her mouth receded as the Uber driver eased the car onto the airport exit. *Where had the time gone?* "Just about."

"Remember to text us when you get to Philadelphia and again when you land in Los Angeles."

"I will. See you in a couple of weeks."

"Okay. Be safe. I love you."

"Love you too," she replied thickly. *I will not cry*, she told herself sternly as she tucked her phone back in her tote. Her tongue grew increasingly dry and lifeless as she watched the terminal loom larger. Minutes later, they were in the Departures lane waiting in line for a curbside opening.

The driver eased the SUV to the curb, shifted into park, turned on the flashers, and then got out of the car. Fingers stiff, Mallory groped for her door handle and met the driver at the back of the vehicle as he lifted the hatch. He set the suitcase on the ground, raised the handle, and spun it to face her.

"Thank you," she said with a travesty of a smile.

A whistle shrilled. "Move along," the traffic officer called out.

"It was my pleasure. Have a good trip."

She nodded, grasping her suitcase handle. The driver pressed the button to close the hatch and hurried to slide back behind the wheel. Mallory turned and faced the terminal entrance. Every fiber of her being seemed to scream in protest as she rolled her suitcase through the automatic door, other travelers rushing past her.

She moved to one side and watched the controlled frenzy of the terminal. *Please, God, help me through this.*

"Nervous about flying?" a middle-aged airline attendant asked sympathetically. "Here, let me help you check your bag and print your boarding pass," he said, escorting Mallory to a kiosk.

Mallory merely smiled, not bothering to correct him.

Easier by far to let him think I'm afraid of flying than to try to explain the real source of my fear, she thought, handing him her travel itinerary.

Minutes later, accepting the baggage claim check and boarding pass from the attendant with a smile, she waited as he wheeled her suitcase to the baggage check-in counter, fastened the self-adhesive destination tag around the suitcase handle, and passed it over to the baggage attendant. She turned and faced the press of humanity being herded like cattle through the security checkpoint. The fingers of her right hand touched the bracelet. Taking a deep breath, she moved her tote bag to her shoulder, Santa's colorful luggage tag swaying gently, and headed to the checkpoint.

Los Angeles

Mallory emerged from the Jetway into Terminal 4 of Los Angeles International Airport and, following the directional signs, headed towards Baggage Claim. She had done it: she had made the cross-country trip from Albany, to Philadelphia, to L.A., alone.

Mom had been right: traveling first class had made the journey much more comfortable. She was relieved that her seatmate on the Philadelphia-to-L.A. flight was an elderly woman who was content to doze most of their time in the air. Mallory had felt the beginnings of a migraine about twenty minutes after taking off from Philadelphia and was in no mood for small talk. She had taken a migraine pill and closed her eyes, resting quietly until at last she felt well enough to read, watch a movie, or look out at the clouds and ponder her future.

She had felt a moment of excitement when the pilot announced that they were preparing for the descent into Los Angeles. Straightening up, she had peered out the window, watching as the Los Angeles skyline with its aura of smog loomed larger. As they had reached the outskirts of the city, she eagerly began searching the ground below. Yes, there it was: SoFi Stadium, home of the Los Angeles Rams. From the air, the stadium was shaped sort of like an old-fashioned teardrop plumb bob. And then they were past the stadium, crossing over the San Diego Freeway, passing Los Angeles International Airport, and flying over the Pacific briefly before banking into a wide U-turn and easing down to the runway.

Now, stepping onto the Down escalator, she pulled out her phone to send a group text to her family:

> Just got off the plane. On my way to pick up my suitcase and find Lettie. See you in 2 weeks. ♥

Once she reached the lower level, she glanced at the monitor to confirm where the luggage from her flight would be delivered, and then joined the passengers who were already huddled around the carousel.

"Mallory?" a voice behind her said.

She spun around. "Lettie!" She and her cousin hugged excitedly.

Lettie pulled back to look at her. "I can't believe you're here!"

"I can't believe she's here," Gareth said for perhaps the fifth time in the past half hour. "I wish we could see her already. It's taking *forever*!"

Gideon, one arm propped against the window frame, cast a smile over his shoulder at his brother before turning back to his study of the hospital parking lot.

Garrison glanced at his watch. "It shouldn't be much longer now."

"Ready to meet her?"

Gideon turned and saw Graham, dressed in aqua scrubs, standing in the waiting room doorway.

"Yes! Finally!" Gareth exclaimed, leaping up to stand next to Graham.

"But shouldn't we wait for Shannon's parents?" Garrison asked as he and Gideon joined Graham and Gareth.

"Shannon's dad called just a minute ago. They're sitting in a long line of construction traffic, and as slowly as things are moving, it could be as much as an hour before they get here. He said there's no sense in you waiting for them. So come on back. She's perfect!"

Garrison put his arm around Graham's shoulders as they headed down the corridor. "How's Shannon doing?"

"Tired but very happy."

"So which name did you go with?" Gideon asked.

"We've decided on Avery, and," said Graham, stopping and glancing at his father, "her middle name is Grace, after Mom."

"Avery Grace... I like it!" Gideon approved.

Garrison blinked back tears as he hugged his second-oldest son. "Your mom would be so proud." He opened up his left arm to draw Gideon and Gareth into the circle of bittersweet praise and thanksgiving.

Wiping his eyes with the thumb and forefinger of one hand, Graham stepped back and pushed open the door to the hospital room. "Come in and meet the newest member of the Locke family."

"She's so tiny!" Gareth exclaimed a few minutes later. Gideon was taking a turn holding Avery, and Gareth had reached out to gently grasp one of her fists between his thumb and forefinger.

Garrison looked at Graham and Shannon. "She's absolutely beautiful."

"We think so, too," Shannon said, sharing a proud smile with Graham.

"It's about time we had a girl in the family," Gideon murmured, kissing the top of her cap-encased head before relinquishing her to Gareth's eager embrace. And in that moment, Gideon had a sudden vision of himself holding his own newborn child.

"So let me get this straight: you made the trip out to see me because of something *Santa* said to you? I don't know whether I should laugh or be mad," Lettie commented, dipping her chopsticks into her container of Chinese take-out.

Mallory swallowed her bite of food and shook her head. "No, *partially* because of him. It's funny: Mom, Dad, Max, and even Aidan have been basically saying the same things to me that Santa did, but I just couldn't or wouldn't accept them. I told myself they meant well but I just wasn't ready or able to do what they were saying. I mean, they're my family, so of course they would be encouraging me to start putting myself out there again. But hearing it from a total stranger, in a slightly different way… Well, once I got over the shock it just really made me think."

"I can't begin to imagine how I would react if some stranger started telling me things about my life. I wonder how he knew."

"Dad thinks he heard different things from our friends and neighbors and pieced it together that way. But even that doesn't explain it all."

"*I* know! Maybe he's the *real* Santa Claus!"

Mallory rolled her eyes. "Next you'll be saying he was an angel in disguise."

"Oh, even better!" she grinned. "Seriously, though, whoever he was, I'm glad he got through to you. I've missed you."

"I've missed you, too." She wrinkled her brow. "But I have to admit, I'm not sure I would have made the trip out here so soon if Mom and Dad hadn't bought the plane tickets."

"Then, here's to Aunt Meredythe and Uncle Roger!" Lettie said gaily, raising her glass and touching it against Mallory's before taking a sip. "All kidding aside, I'm glad you're here. It's been *ages* since we've spent much time together."

"Hey, *you're* the one who decided to move clear across the country."

"Believe me, looking back, I'm as surprised as you are. After I got my bachelor's degree, I thought I'd stay in upstate New York all my life."

Mallory took a sip of water and carefully set her glass down on the coaster that protected the espresso-colored dining table. "So why *did* you move? What made you decide to give up the scholarship at Albany and come to Los Angeles?"

Using her chopsticks, Lettie prodded the food in her take-out container wordlessly. After a moment, she released the chopsticks and set the container down with a sigh. "Why does any otherwise-smart girl pull up her roots and transplant herself 3,000 miles away from her friends and family? I thought I was in love."

"Really? I had no idea."

"Well, you were sort of preoccupied, and I was… smitten, as Grandma would say. He was in one of my classes, but things didn't really grow beyond friendship until the last semester of undergraduate school. Then he found out he'd been accepted into a master's program at USC and would be starting his classes in the summer, and he made the comment—just in passing, and probably not even expecting me to take him up on it—that I should apply for a master's program out here to be near him." She laughed wryly. "I latched on to that. I was positive it meant he wanted to marry me. I wasn't interested in going to USC, but I did some research and found the Pollard Institute. Their program is accredited and highly rated, so it seemed like the perfect option." She raked the fingers of her right hand through her chestnut hair and sighed. "Believe me, I understand when you talk about well-meaning family… my parents tried to convince me I was making a mistake, that I was sacrificing everything I had going for me at Albany for a half-promise, but I was determined. I guess I had deluded myself into thinking that he was only a *secondary* reason why I was changing schools. Anyway, I applied, was accepted, and came all the way out here only to find out he was already in a serious relationship with someone else."

"Oh, Lettie, no!"

"It was partially my fault. I wanted to surprise him so I never let on that I was transferring out here. I like to think that he would have clued me in if he'd known what I was planning."

"Why didn't you just come back home?"

Pensively, she ran her finger around the rim of her glass. "Too much pride, I guess. I'd burned the bridge with Albany. And, with you back in Hepton Grove, I felt like I'd lost my best friend."

Tears pooled in Mallory's eyes. "I am *so* sorry."

Lettie leaned forward. "Don't be. I liked my classes, and I'd already uprooted to come out here, so it just seemed easier to stay." She looked at Mallory diffidently. "And now I've started dating someone else. His name is Ethan, and, well, so far he seems pretty special," she said softly.

Impulsively, Mallory clasped Lettie's hands. "I'm so happy for you. I can't wait to meet him."

"You'll meet him tomorrow night," she said eagerly. "We're going to show you some of the sights. In fact—" Her phone pinged and she peeked at the screen. "It's my mom. I'd better take this."

"Of course. Give her my love." Mallory pushed back from the table and walked two steps into the diminutive living room. She looked around at the small apartment assessingly. Black, white, and stainless steel. *Has California really changed Lettie's taste this much?*

Noticing the sliding door, she opened it and stepped outside. The balcony was underwhelming—no more than a small foothold, really. At most, a few flower pots or perhaps two tiny bistro chairs might fit in the space if angled just so. She leaned against the aluminum railing and looked down at the cars that jockeyed for position in the late rush-hour race. Driving from the airport to Lettie's apartment, she'd been unimpressed with L.A.—she disliked the noise, the smog, the traffic, the air of entitlement so many people seemed to radiate. Although she still had not revised her first impression, she recalled that she'd had similar reactions the first time she'd visited Albany and New York City. The place wasn't important; it was being with Lettie that mattered.

Named Letitia after her maternal grandmother, Lettie was the only child of Mallory's uncle, Donald Glencoe and his wife Kaye. Until Mallory and her family had relocated from Wisconsin, they had seen Lettie and her parents just once a year, when the extended Glencoe clan would reunite for Easter at the family homestead in New York's Finger Lakes region. The children were expected to be on their best behavior at these gatherings, so their interactions tended to be stilted and subdued.

Roger and Meredythe's move to Hepton Grove changed all that. Hepton Grove was not quite an hour from Donald and Kaye's home in Saratoga Springs, and the two families made a point of getting together every couple of weeks, giving the cousins a chance to become better acquainted. Although Lettie had grown up a child of financial privilege—Donald was a prominent attorney in the Albany area; Kaye, a .com heiress, ran a regional nonprofit organization; and

Grandma Letitia had endowed an investment account to cover Lettie's higher education costs—Mallory had rarely envied her cousin. Instead, from age six when the girls had their first sleepover at Lettie's house, Mallory had sensed the loneliness behind Lettie's excitement at having an overnight guest. Mallory tried to imagine what life would be like without Max or Aidan, and her tender heart was touched. By the end of that weekend, the cousins had cemented a bond that neither time nor distance apart could diminish.

As fourteen-year-olds, the cousins had first devised the plan to live together and go to college. However, during their junior year of high school, when the girls were starting to visit college campuses, Lettie's Grandma Letitia had suddenly stepped in. Although Lettie was an excellent student, she couldn't seem to settle on a career—too many things seemed to interest her. Since Letitia was footing the bill for Lettie's education, she wanted Lettie to look at colleges in Florida, where she could keep tabs on her granddaughter and make sure Lettie wasn't frittering away her time and Letitia's money. No granddaughter of hers was going to drift along like the grandchildren of some of her friends had, changing majors repeatedly until they were almost thirty when they finally graduated. No, the girls could wait until graduate school to live together, Letitia had said consolingly, and Lettie had acquiesced.

Mallory was disappointed, but she understood.

So the cousins had gone to separate colleges for their bachelor's programs, but always with the goal of pursuing their master's degrees at the same institution. Like Mallory, Lettie had decided to major in architecture, but while Mallory was primarily interested in residential architecture, Lettie was drawn to industrial design. Everything was on track: the girls were scheduled to graduate and they had already received provisional acceptance into a master's program at Albany.

Until the events of nearly two years ago…

Lettie's words echoed in her mind: "I felt like I'd lost my best friend."

Mallory raised her eyes to look off towards the Los Angeles skyline, and felt a new depth of gratitude to her parents for sending her out here. Somehow she would find a way to make up to Lettie for the past two years.

She gradually swept her gaze around to face the building across the street from Lettie's apartment. Panic rose like bile when she noticed three young men—one directly opposite her, one on the top floor and two units to the left, and the other one floor down and a unit to the right—regarding her with varying degrees of interest from their respective balconies. The young man on the top floor raised a hand to draw her attention.

Suddenly short of breath, she spun around and reeled back into the apartment. *Safe*, she thought as she slid the door closed and turned the lock. She rested a minute, one hand still pressed against the door as she steadied herself. Santa's words repeated in her mind, as they had so often in the past weeks: "That's fear talking."

Instinctively, her fingers reached for the bracelet and spun it slowly as she silently spoke the two verses engraved on it.

"I love you too, Mom," Lettie was saying. "Give Dad a kiss for me… Yes, I sure will. Bye." She ended the call and placed the phone beside her. "Mom wanted to make sure you had arrived all right. She sends her love."

Roused from her mental recitations, Mallory managed a smile and a nod as she moved away from the sliding door.

"Are you all right?" Lettie asked.

"I'm fine," Mallory said, rejoining her cousin at the table. She changed the subject. "So when did you move *here*? I thought you had a roommate?"

"*Had* is the operative word. She got a small part on one episode of a TV show a couple of months ago and decided to quit college to concentrate on her acting career. Her agent, or whatever he is, told her she needs to get away from the college scene and live with someone who has similar ambitions, so she broke the lease. I didn't have anyone else I was comfortable living with, so I had to move out, too."

"Oh, that's too bad."

"Fortunately I was able to sublet this furnished studio for a few months while I try to find a new place closer to Pollard, but I'm paying a fortune in storage fees in the meantime."

"Well, I hope you can find a new place soon. I'll be glad to tag along while you look."

"Good—I was hoping you wouldn't mind going with me while you're here."

"Not at all."

"So what are *your* plans now that you won't be working full-time at the clinic anymore?"

"Actually, I'm thinking about finally getting my master's degree."

"You mean you're going back to—"

"Oh, no," Mallory cut in quickly. "No, if I do this, I'm going to apply somewhere else."

"Wow! That must have been some talk you had with Santa! So where are you applying?"

"I haven't decided yet. Remember, I said I was only *thinking* about getting my degree," she said with a smile.

"Point taken. You know," Lettie continued, "the Pollard Institute has just added a master's program for historical preservation. Maybe you should look into that. I would be shocked if you didn't get in." She cocked her head and shot a speculative look at her cousin. "So what do you say, Mallory? We could share an apartment just like we planned all those years ago!"

"Oh, Lettie, I'm only here for a short visit. I have no desire to move out here."

"That's what you say now. We'll see if that changes after a week or two," she replied mischievously.

Mallory merely smiled and shook her head.

CHAPTER 7

Thursday, January 10th
Los Angeles

Mallory's eyes fluttered open. She lay there for a moment, momentarily disoriented by the pre-dawn traffic noises, the soft chime of an elevator, the narrowness of her bed. And then she remembered: Lettie's apartment.

She turned on her side, reached for her phone, and sighed: 4:33 a.m.—7:33 a.m. back home. Well, at least she had slept a *little* longer than yesterday.

She lifted her head and looked at the sleeping form of her cousin, burrowed under the sheet and blanket of the sofa bed. Mallory quietly slipped from the twin-sized mattress of the convertible chair, drew out her laptop from her carry-on tote, and settled with it at the dining table.

After connecting to Lettie's wireless network, she accessed her Gmail account and started a group email to her family.

> Well, as you can see from the timestamp of this email, I still have not adjusted to Pacific Time, even though this will be my second full day in Los Angeles. Yesterday, I tagged along while Lettie attended a couple of her classes. I have to say, I was impressed by the campus and its facilities, and her professors seem very good.
>
> Last night Lettie and her boyfriend Ethan took me on a night tour of the city, which was fun even though it was drizzling. I'm beginning to understand why Lettie seems to like it here.

Ethan is very nice—very low-key, very down-to-earth, unlike some of the people I saw on campus yesterday. He apparently works for his mom part-time while finishing up his master's in marketing. He and Lettie are a good fit—I wouldn't be surprised if he turns out to be The One.

We're going back to campus today for one of her classes and then I'll be on my own for a couple of hours while she meets with some classmates to work on a project. After that, Ethan is going to take us around to look at a couple of apartments for Lettie, so I'll have a chance to see more of the city.

Lettie is still pushing for me to apply to the Pollard Institute. She's brought it up a couple of times in the past day and a half, and I'm sure she'll mention it again. She is relentless! LOL!

My love to you all. Talk to you soon.

———————————————

At nine-thirty, Lettie and Mallory exited the classroom and walked side-by-side down the hall.

"So I'll meet you at the library?" Lettie asked, stopping in front of a studio.

"Yes."

"They have a café on the second floor. Why don't you go there—it'll be easier to find you."

"Okay, sounds good."

"See you in about an hour," Lettie said, entering the studio.

Mallory carried her cup of coffee to a small table by the window overlooking the courtyard. Placing her tote on the chair next to her, she pulled out her laptop and powered it on as she took a sip. She did a Google search on "Pollard Institute Los Angeles." Clicking the link to the institute's home page, she began to read.

> The Talbot C. Pollard Institute for Industrial, Architectural, and Interior Design—affectionately called *The Pollard* by students and faculty alike—is a fresh, innovative, fully accredited institution of higher education. Founded in 2010 in memory of award-winning architect and educator Talbot C. Pollard, the institute has grown steadily in both student population and the array of courses and programs available for study.
>
> The campus covers approximately 40 acres and currently consists of an administration building that also holds the campus bookstore and Portfolio—the name of the faculty/staff dining room; a student activity center that features a fitness center, a climbing wall, a food court, and a game room; a library with private and small-group study rooms; and two classroom/studio/office buildings: one dedicated to Industrial Design and the other accommodating the Architectural and Interior Design Departments. A sixth building—which will house classrooms, studios, and faculty offices for the newly created Historic Preservation and Restoration Department—is scheduled for completion this March.

Mallory clicked the Academic Degrees tab and selected Master of Arts. Sure enough, the web page displayed a banner announcing the coming launch of the new Master of Arts in Historic Preservation. She read the bio of the department chairman, Dr. Frederick Ames. *Impressive.* But a review of the out-of-state tuition and fees was sobering. *Unless I get a part-time job somewhere, there's no way I could afford this.*

She closed her eyes, tilted her head forward slightly, and whispered the words of Psalm 143:8, one of the Bible verses that had served as a daily prayer over the years: "Let the morning bring me word of your unfailing love, for I have put my trust in you. Show me the way I should go, for to You I entrust my life."

After a moment, she opened her eyes and turned back to her laptop. She clicked a link and, tentatively at first and then with growing confidence, began typing an email.

However, it wasn't until the next morning, when she returned to the Pollard Institute for the appointments she had made—first with Dr. Ames, then with an admissions counselor, and finally with the director of the institute's library—that staying in Los Angeles herself seemed possible. Encouraged by those meetings, she called Max, hoping to catch him before his next class of the day.

"So it would be… what, a year-and-a-half tops to get your degree?" he asked after listening to her summary of the meetings.

"Yes."

"Well, I wish you could be closer to home, but it's not forever—assuming you haven't changed your mind about opening your own architectural design firm back here?"

"No, that's still my plan."

"Then do it," he'd told her. "You have nothing to lose. And I know Lettie would be glad to have you move in with her."

So, buoyed by Max's encouraging words, she spent the rest of that rainy morning in the library, where she completed and submitted the application for admission. She then contacted the registrar of her school in Albany and requested that copies of her transcripts be sent electronically to the Pollard Institute's office of admissions.

CHAPTER 8

Eight months later: Sunday, October 20ᵗʰ
Los Angeles

Laptop tote slung over one shoulder, Mallory stepped off the city bus and paused, enjoying the 70-degree warmth of this day. It was hard to believe that a week ago, while she was home in Hepton Grove for fall break, the temperatures had struggled to reach the 40s. But it was harder still to believe that she was here in Los Angeles, attending college.

Smiling ruefully, she cast her mind back to January, when she had embarked on her visit to Lettie. How convinced she'd been that she would return home from her two-week visit unchanged, ready to pick up her life in Hepton Grove; how determined she'd been to persuade Lettie to move back east—never dreaming that *she* would be the one persuaded to move.

Lettie had been ecstatic when she learned Mallory had applied for admission. "This is a game-changer," she'd declared, and had immediately insisted on searching for a two-bedroom apartment that afternoon. Mallory told Lettie it was premature, but Lettie had disagreed.

"Look, I can afford to pay for a two-bedroom apartment by myself for six months or so and by then we'll know if you've gotten in. Worst case scenario, they deny you admission and you either apply somewhere else, or you move back home and I have to find a new roommate. But I'll be shocked if you aren't accepted. So let's find a place we both like and go from there."

But it was Lettie's boyfriend, Ethan, who had pointed them to the modest 7-story apartment building located about 15 miles from campus and about the same distance from Ethan's house. Originally built in the 1970s, the building consisted of a wide central section with two narrower wings jutting out at a forty-five degree angle on either side. The apartment in question was on the fourth floor of the building's right-hand wing and measured a little less than 1200 square feet. Facing north, it overlooked the parking lot and thus was much quieter than those that fronted the street. While the complex had fewer amenities than similar-sized properties, the girls felt that the abundant square footage and updated finishes of the apartment plus its in-unit washer and dryer more than compensated for the lack of a fitness center or roof-top deck. They had signed the lease on the spot, committing to take possession on the first of February.

Mallory had flown home on January 22nd and, after a frenzied week of sorting, boxing, and packing, had returned to Los Angeles on the 30th. Two days later, Ethan had arrived with a rental truck. After loading up Mallory's suitcase and tote bag and Lettie's few belongings from the studio apartment, the three of them had emptied out Lettie's storage unit, which not only held Lettie's bedroom and living room furniture but also contained the bedroom, dining, and kitchen items Mallory had bought after she and Lettie had signed their lease. The next day, in anticipation of receiving her sewing machine, which was among the personal items she'd ask her parents to ship to her, Mallory and Lettie visited a fabric store. By the end of that first week, the apartment was fully furnished and decorated.

And now, here it was October, with just over six weeks left in the fall semester. Mallory missed her family and friends back home, but between her classwork, her part-time job at the institute's library, plus spending time with Lettie, her days were very full.

Her phone rang and she smiled when she saw Max's name.

"Hi!"

"Hi, sis. Where are you? I hear traffic noises."

"I just got back from campus. I had to work a couple of hours at the library this morning."

"Oh, I see. I guess you're excited about going to your first professional football game today."

"You have a knack for stating the obvious," she teased, tugging on one of the tall glass doors to the apartment building.

"Ouch! Well, I'll be looking for you on TV tonight. I suppose you'll be the one wearing a ball gown and fur stole since you'll be in a fancy suite."

"Very funny. It's an end-zone suite, right above field level. And while it's true we won't be wearing our Rams jerseys since we'll be going out to dinner afterwards, Lettie confirmed with Ethan's mom that it's fine to wear jeans—no business casual attire required."

"Well, that's good. At least you'll be comfortable. And seriously, how lucky to be in a suite! That doesn't happen every day."

Mallory waved to the woman behind the concierge desk and pressed the Up elevator button. "Tell me about it. It was so nice of them to invite me to tag along. What about you? Are you going to watch the game with some of your buddies?"

"Actually, I'm at home. Mom, Dad, and I are going to Aidan and Phoebe's for the game. We're already warming up. Go, Giants! Boo, Rams!"

She rolled her eyes but, not rising to the bait, merely asked, "Don't you have class tomorrow?"

"Yeah, but I figure I'll just spend the night at home and then get up early in the morning and drive to campus."

"*Very* early."

"As long as I'm on the road by five, I should be fine."

"Well, be safe. Give my love to everyone. I miss you!"

"I miss you, too. Bye, Mal. And remember: be bold!"

She pushed away the pang of homesickness that suddenly assailed her as she hung up and tucked her phone back in her tote bag. The elevator doors opened and she hitched the tote more securely on her shoulder before stepping into the hallway.

"Lettie?" Mallory called out, closing the apartment door behind her.

Lettie bustled out of her bedroom. "Oh, thank goodness you're home. Ethan will be here in about ten minutes."

"Already?" she asked, setting her keys on the console table and turning to look at her cousin. Lettie's worried face alarmed her. "What's wrong?"

"Ethan's grandmother fell and she's being taken to the hospital. We're going to meet his parents there and stay until we know how she is."

Mallory swallowed her disappointment. "Oh, I'm so sorry to hear that. Just do whatever you need to—don't worry about me. Maybe we can go to a game another time."

"No, we'll drop you off at the stadium before we head over—we just need to leave earlier than we'd originally planned. Ethan said his parents won't be going to the game or to dinner, but with luck he and I will be able to join you for the second half. Depending on how his grandmother is, we'll probably drop you back off here after the game and then head back to the hospital."

"I don't know, Lettie…"

Lettie pulled a light jacket from the coat rack near the door. "Look, Ethan said it's a suite that his parents share with some friends of his family. These friends apparently travel a lot and rarely attend the games, so odds are you'll be in the suite all by yourself until we can get there. *Please* don't change your mind about going. I would hate to think I ruined this for you."

"You haven't ruined anything. I'm just glad you're able to be there to support Ethan and his parents." She continued to look at her cousin hesitantly. "You aren't trying to set me up with someone, are you?"

"No! I promise! I just want you to have some *fun* for a change. You know the saying: 'All work and no play makes Jane—'"

"—a dull girl," Mallory said in unison with her cousin. "Okay, point taken." She picked up her laptop tote. "Let me drop this off in my room and change real quick, and I should be ready when Ethan gets here."

Lettie hugged her impulsively. "Thank you for not backing out!"

Forty minutes later, Mallory stepped out of Ethan's car, one of the suite passes clutched in her hand. With a quick wave, she closed the door, and Ethan and Lettie sped off towards the medical center.

Mallory turned and surveyed the stadium where groups of people converged towards the various entrances. Although modern architecture was not her favorite style, the structure was striking, the large

Karen Lail

graduated pillars supporting the fluid curves of the transparent roof, giving a light, open-air feeling. *Like a colonnade*, she thought.

Two couples brushed past either side of her and, suddenly overwhelmed by the crowd, she stepped closer to the edge of the walkway leading to the VIP entrance Ethan had pointed out to her. She folded her arms tightly against herself. It would be so easy—so much safer—to just turn around, flag down a taxi, and head back to the apartment. But when she had moved out here to join Lettie, she had resolved to try to be more open, to emulate Max's adventurous spirit to some degree. "Be bold," Max had said at the end of their conversation less than an hour ago.

She straightened up. *Okay, bold it is.* With that, she joined the line of spectators who waited to pass through security.

Noticing Mallory's air of uncertainty, a member of the event staff offered to direct her to the suite, and gratefully she showed him her pass. A floor-to-ceiling window and full glass panel door marked the suite's entrance. A server met her as she approached and asked if Mallory wanted to order a beverage and some food. Requesting a glass of lemonade, she pushed open the door. As Lettie had predicted, Mallory was the only one in the suite. Two television monitors were affixed to one side wall; below the monitors hung a small wall-mounted table. Midway up the opposite wall, a row of mirrors stretched front to back, reflecting the monitors and the light from the field-facing end of the suite.

The server returned and, laying her jacket on the table, Mallory pulled some money from her cross-body purse and paid and tipped the girl for the lemonade. Drawn to the front of the room, Mallory carried her glass to the window that overlooked the field. Secure in her anonymity, she looked around her with interest. A doorway to her right led outside to the bar and stools allocated to the suite. In front of the bar, facing out to the field, was an upholstered sofa large enough to accommodate up to four adults comfortably. No doubt, that was where she, Lettie, and Ethan would spend the majority of the game.

For now, though, she preferred to stay inside and observe from her vantage point.

The stadium thrummed with energy and anticipation. Some spectators were laughing, others appeared to be arguing good-naturedly, children bounced up and down with excitement, and food vendors hawked their wares. There was just as much activity on the field where, just minutes from now, at 4:05 p.m. local time, the Giants would square off against the Rams. Officials strode up and down the sidelines, cheerleaders moved briskly in sync to the music that flooded the stadium, and television cameras panned the stands, their feed displayed on the massive dual-sided Oculus suspended above the field. Exhilaration surged within her. She began clapping as first the Giants and then the Rams ran onto the field, and she laughed softly just from the thrill of being at this game.

The soft whoosh of the door opening behind her and a male voice saying, "Root beer, please," drew her attention. A blond-haired young man of about her age had entered the suite and the server was bustling away to fill his order.

Alarmed, Mallory ceased in mid-clap and lowered her hands as her eyes locked on his.

"Where are Bill and Kendra?" he demanded, pausing at the table as if afraid to venture any further. Before Mallory could answer, his eyes narrowed and he added, "Are you Ethan's girlfriend?"

Bewildered by the look of suspicion on the stranger's face, she said, "They're all at the hospital. Ethan's grandmother fell. He and Lettie—that's my cousin, Ethan's girlfriend—hope to—"

"Oh, no, I wish I'd known," he cut in, hunching a shoulder.

"—be here for the second half," she trailed off, her panic yielding to affront. Taking a small sip of lemonade, she turned back to the window and pretended to scan the stands to her left as she tried not to feel slighted. *I knew this was a mistake.*

Gideon pulled out his phone and quickly punched a number. Ethan answered right away.

"Hey, I was able to get away after all," Gideon said quietly, turning away towards the suite entrance. "I'm at the stadium now. Are you coming?"

"Not until maybe half-time. Grandma fell and we're all at the hospital to make sure she's okay. So go on to the suite. Lettie's cousin is there and can keep you company. Just go easy with her—she's a little shy."

He cast a glance over his shoulder at the girl's rigid back. "Okay. Hope your grandma is all right. See you later." *Good, the story checks out*, he thought as he pocketed his phone. He looked up as the server carried in his drink. "Thank you," he said with a smile, handing her some money. "Keep the change." *Now to appease Lettie's cousin.* He turned back towards the girl and watched with alarm as she suddenly spun away from the window, plunked down her almost-full glass, snatched up her jacket and, eyes downcast, started charging past him. "Wait," he said, reaching out towards her.

She recoiled as if she'd been scalded, but she stopped. After a beat she cut her eyes up at him.

"You don't need to go."

She drew in a ragged breath. "Yes, I think I do. You obviously think I'm intruding."

"You're not intruding. You have every right to be here."

"Only because Ethan vouched for me."

He couldn't deny it. He searched for something to say that would placate her, but came up empty. "Stay," he said desperately.

She shook her head and started to move past him, but the announcer intervened: "Ladies and gentlemen, please rise for our national anthem." The girl stopped again. She sighed and, folding her jacket over her left arm, moved back to the window overlooking the field and placed her hand over her heart. Gideon assumed the same stance.

When the cheers following the anthem died down, he took a step closer as she unzipped her purse to retrieve her phone. "Really— don't go. Ethan would have my head if he knew I'd upset you. Please?"

She looked up at him wordlessly.

"Please?" he repeated.

She studied him a moment longer and then, releasing the phone, gave a slight nod and picked up her glass of lemonade instead.

He gestured for her to precede him to the outside seats.

Once outside, she hesitated as she looked at the sofa and then moved to the furthest bar stool.

Well, maybe I can get her to forgive me by half-time, he thought.

She cast a glance up at him as he settled on the stool at the opposite end of the bar and then she looked pointedly away.

His lips curved ruefully. *Or not.*

While Mallory intently followed the action of the game, a part of her brain continued to fume over the rude young man. She found it odd that he hadn't introduced himself, but she wasn't about to volunteer her name. He seemed to be curious about her—she felt, rather than saw, each time that he peeked at her—but he didn't try to engage her in conversation.

Good thing.

Or was it?

"It's one of the smaller end-zone suites that his parents share with some friends of his family," Lettie had said. If Ethan was friends with this guy, then Ethan would tend to side with him.

And Lettie would be placed in a very difficult position: torn between her loyalty to Mallory and her growing fondness for her boyfriend.

I need to take a step back. Casting a surreptitious look at the young man, she considered the moment of their meeting from *his* point of view: walking into the suite that *his* family had helped pay for, only to find a strange girl there, alone, claiming to be Ethan's girlfriend's cousin. *If the situation was reversed, I'd want to check out his story, too.*

Her conscience pricked her. She'd overreacted, plain and simple. *Now, how to make it up to him?* She struggled to overcome her natural reticence, to find a way to break the wall of ice she'd erected between them, but it wasn't until near the end of the first quarter while shaking her head over a pass-interference call that she allowed her eyes to meet his.

"Bad call," he remarked promptly, almost as though he'd been waiting—hoping?—for her to look his way.

"It sure was—at least from this angle."

"Ah, well, overall the referees have done a good job, so I guess we can't complain too much."

"That's true—and at least it's only the second down."

"Yeah, they still have time to make up the yards."

The topic exhausted, Mallory nodded and was about to watch the replay on the Oculus, but he forestalled her. "You know, this is kind of awkward—you over there, and me over here. Would you mind if I sat next to you?"

She looked over her shoulder at him and shrugged. "No, I guess not."

He perched on the stool next to hers.

After a moment, Mallory turned to him resolutely. "I'm sorry I acted so rudely earlier. It was bad form on my part."

"I think we were both caught off guard. I hope you can forgive me, too."

"Of course," she said with a shy smile.

"By the way," he said, holding out his hand, "my name's Gideon."

Gideon, Mallory repeated silently, feeling an elusive sense of recognition. She eased her hand into his, its warm strength oddly comforting. "I'm Mallory."

"How do you do?" they said, almost in unison. They continued to smile at each other uncertainly for a moment and then, flustered, Mallory drew her hand away and looked back at the field.

They watched as the official walked off the penalty and placed the ball on the Rams' thirty-third yard line. The players lined up on either side, the ball was snapped, and the quarterback threw, just missing connection with the intended receiver.

At that moment, their server stopped next to them. "Can I bring you some fresh drinks?"

Gideon looked at Mallory, who nodded. "Yes, please. And maybe some chips and salsa—" he said, and then turned again to Mallory. "Unless you'd prefer something else?"

"Chips and salsa sounds great. But could I have a Coke instead of lemonade this time?"

"You sure can. I'll be right back."

As the game went on, they chatted now and then, to comment on various plays or to fill the breaks in action when a time-out was called. Despite Gideon's self-confident demeanor, Mallory sensed that he was rather shy and wary, too, so she made more of an effort than she ordinarily would to not only respond (as good manners dictated) but also to volunteer remarks of her own. With each exchange, she found herself becoming more and more comfortable in his company—and more and more convinced that she had seen or met him somewhere before. *Stop it!* she told herself sternly. Since she'd come to L.A., she was constantly seeing people who reminded her in some way of friends or family back home. That was undoubtedly the case here.

As the ball was being turned over on downs with less than two minutes left in the half, Gideon looked over at her in wonder. "I can't believe you really like football. Most of the girls I know don't particularly care for it."

"Call it survival. My father and brothers love the game, so I had to either learn to enjoy it too, or go absolutely crazy."

He laughed. "So who's your favorite team?"

"Oh, that's hard to say. We lived in Wisconsin for a couple of years after I was born, so, like my Dad, I'm partial to Green Bay. But I also like the Rams. My brother Max gives me a hard time about that."

"So your family lives here now?"

"No, actually, they're in a little town in upstate New York. I think that's part of my attraction to this particular game: New York versus L.A., my old home against my new one—or temporary one, anyway. I came out here to get my master's degree." *I can't believe I'm talking this much,* she thought.

He grinned. "It'll be interesting to see which one wins." He looked at the field again as a group of about 40 teenagers came out on the field. "I guess this is the half-time entertainment."

The announcer introduced the award-winning dance troupe and their performance "Dance Fascination." The teenagers lined up on either sideline, and as each successive song in the medley played, four or five from each side would rotate onto the field to perform their portion of the routine.

"These kids are really great," Gideon commented, and Mallory nodded her agreement. As the group performing to "Dance, Dance, Dance" by the Beach Boys exited the field, the opening beats of "Can't Help but Dance" sounded, a song Mallory hadn't heard in quite a few years.

The clock on the wall goes tock-tick-tock
My feet tap in time while the teacher talks.
Leap from my seat as the clock strikes three,
Slide across the floor upon one knee.
Can't help but dance!
Head and shoulders, hips, knees, and feet
Twist and jive to the pulsing beat.
Dash down the hall and spin out the door
Grab my girl and whirl some more
Can't help but dance!

"That brings back memories," she murmured, more to herself than to Gideon.

"For me, too," he said, chuckling, the fingers of his left hand tapping the side of his cup.

Mallory stared at his hands, watching his fingers drumming in time to the music. Drumming. Her eyes flew to his face and scanned his features, mentally changing his blond hair to light brown, and then she looked away. *Now* she knew why he had seemed familiar: Gideon was *Gideon Locke*, idol of her mid-teens. He and his three brothers had written and originally recorded the song that was playing. The years that had elapsed had thinned his face, and he was taller in person than he had appeared in photographs or onstage, but it was Gideon Locke all the same. When she was a teenager, Mallory used to dream about meeting Gideon, imagining what he would say, and mentally scripting out all the witty and entrancing responses she would make in return. *So much for "witty and entrancing."* Now, sitting next to her erstwhile teenage crush, she realized with regret how different she was from her younger self; how lost were the naiveté, the blithe optimism, the rosy dreams of her early-to-mid teens. The irony struck her bitterly: Only a moment before, she'd congratulated herself on feeling so relaxed; now she could only look at him hesitantly, miserably, before turning away, toying with the rim of her soda glass as she wondered what to say or do next.

"By the way," he said casually, although his eyes sparkled with mischief, "you never told me your last name."

Drawing back from her bleak thoughts, she glanced at him. "It's Glencoe."

He turned and laid his left arm across the back of Mallory's stool as he held out his right hand. "Well, once again, I'm very pleased to meet you, Mallory Glencoe."

Despite the fact that his fingertips rested lightly against her shoulder, she didn't feel the usual urge to pull away when someone outside the family touched her. Rather, recalling footage she had seen years ago of screaming fans chasing him and his brothers, she was more concerned that others might recognize him and they would be mobbed. Casting a glance around at the people in the neighboring suites, she leaned toward him as she rested her hand in his. "And I'm pleased to meet you, Gideon Locke," she said softly.

Again Gideon chuckled, and he squeezed her hand slightly before releasing it. "I *thought* you recognized me just now," he said, keeping his voice low. "You got all tense and then looked at me like I was an ogre."

"Not an ogre! I just didn't know what to say to you, if anything."

"I know, so I thought I'd make things easier for you," he teased.

"So 'easy' that I almost *choked* when you asked me my last name."

"I believe it. You should have seen your face!"

"I can imagine," she replied, smiling. "So when did you go blond?" she asked, gesturing at his hair.

"Right before this game." He leaned closer. "Is wig—part of disguise," he said with a terrible foreign accent, and then grinned at her peal of laughter.

That interchange marked a subtle change. No longer were they two strangers who happened to be sitting side-by-side at the game. The rapport they'd established, in addition to their mutual liking for football, seemed to take them beyond that. Or so it seemed to Mallory.

Gideon stood up. "Well, half-time is almost over. I'm going to stretch my legs for a bit and maybe check in with Ethan. Can I bring you anything?"

"No, but I'll walk with you as far as the ladies' room," she replied, picking up her purse.

Karen Lail

The ladies' room for the field suites was being serviced when they reached it.

"I guess I'll try the next one," Mallory commented.

"I'll walk with you."

He moved slightly ahead to forge a path through the press of spectators milling about. By the time they'd reached the next set of restrooms, the line on the women's side was fairly short, but still much longer than the queue outside the men's room.

"I'll see you later," Mallory said before heading to take a place in line.

CHAPTER 9

When she emerged from the ladies' room, she saw Gideon standing a few feet away, chatting with a couple of young women near the water fountains.

Mallory hesitated. *Should I join him? Just wait here?*

No. She had no claim on Gideon—the last thing she wanted to do was to insinuate herself into his conversation. It was clear from their laughter and their shining eyes that Gideon was keeping the girls well entertained. As a celebrity, Gideon must have learned long ago how to be charming—which meant that any connection between them Mallory may have felt, any rapport she'd imagined they'd established was surely just in her mind. She chided herself for being so naïve, then straightened up, resolved to withdraw with grace. Just as she was turning to walk away, Gideon noticed her, and an odd expression— almost of relief—flitted across his face. He gestured towards Mallory as he said something to the girls, and then he turned and jogged over to join her.

"I was afraid I'd missed you," he said. "I talked to Ethan, and he said he and Lettie are on their way and should be here in about fifteen minutes."

"Good. Hopefully that means his grandmother isn't too seriously hurt."

He nodded. "I know." Putting his hands in his pockets, he hunched his shoulders slightly to bring his mouth closer to her ear and asked, "Would you mind if we took the long way back to our suite?"

Eager to see more of the stadium, she replied, "Not at all."

Gideon smiled and they turned the opposite way. Occasionally as they walked, Gideon's body would brush against hers as he moved to let someone pass, and several times he stopped and turned to the side facing into her, whether to shield her or to hide his face, Mallory could not be certain.

His phone pinged and, pulling it from his back pocket, he read the message on the screen. "Oh, Ethan and Lettie are here. I guess we'd better hurry and meet them."

Lettie and Ethan stood up to greet them when they entered the field suite a few minutes later. Ethan and Gideon shared a man hug, and then Ethan introduced Lettie to Gideon.

"Ethan and I have known each other for ages—Kendra, his mom, is our publicist," Gideon explained.

"Oh, wow—I had no idea," Lettie said, shooting a why-didn't-you-tell-me look at her boyfriend before shaking Gideon's hand.

"Yeah, ever since I've known them, I've never felt like an only child—they treat me like family."

"That's because you are," Gideon asserted. "That's why Gareth wanted you to be one of his groomsmen."

"Speaking of family… how's your grandmother?" Mallory asked.

"She has a broken wrist and a couple of cracked ribs, and she apparently hit her head pretty hard, but fortunately there's no concussion. Because of her age, the doctor wants her to stay overnight for observation, but she should be able to go home sometime tomorrow morning."

"I'm so glad," Mallory said.

"Yeah, that's great, Ethan. She's a special lady," Gideon stated.

A roar from the field drew their attention, and they saw the Giants and Rams emerging from their respective tunnels. The two couples remained standing to watch the kick-off and reception that launched the second half and then Ethan took Lettie by the hand and led her to the far end of the sofa. Gideon gestured for Mallory to follow, and she settled between him and Lettie.

The rest of the game seemed to pass swiftly. In the final minutes of the game, the Rams were ahead 17 to 10. The Giants had possession and were in range of scoring another touchdown when they fumbled the ball and the Rams recovered. Three downs later, the Rams still had not crossed the 50-yard line. Instead of punting, the Rams surprised and delighted the crowd by lining up to run the ball one more time. The ball was snapped; the quarterback dropped back, started to throw, ran to avoid an oncoming Giant, and managed to release the ball just before being tackled. Gideon and Mallory jumped up to watch as the ball arced perfectly into the receiver's outstretched hands. As the receiver gathered the ball against him and carried it triumphantly over the goal line, Gideon startled Mallory by pulling her to him in an ecstatic hug. "They did it!" he exclaimed. "Wasn't that pass *fantastic?*" he cried, tightening his hold on her in his excitement.

"It sure was," she agreed breathlessly, resisting the instinct to stiffen up. He released her and reached behind her to give Ethan a high-five.

Although others in the stadium had already started filing out now that it was clear the Rams had won, the four of them stayed to watch the Rams score the point after touchdown and then kick off to the Giants. A Giants player caught and held the ball as the clock ran down.

"Three—two—one... That's it! That's the game!" Gideon exclaimed, hugging her again. And, as he released her, Mallory felt a pang of sorrow that the game *had* ended. Despite its rocky start, it had been one of the most enjoyable afternoons she'd had since she'd come to L.A. As she watched Gideon shrug into his jacket, it struck her: she was lonely. Even though she and Lettie shared an apartment and went to the same college, they rarely saw each other. Their classes were on different days, Mallory had her job at the library, and Lettie understandably spent most of her free time with Ethan. Occasionally, Lettie and Ethan tried to include her in some of their activities, but she would tag along only if it was something she could afford or, as with this football game, a ticket would otherwise go unused—and always with the stipulation that they *not* try to set her up with someone. Meeting Gideon today had obviously been as much a surprise to him as it had been to her, and perhaps *because* there were no expectations from either of them, she had enjoyed his company, if for no other reason than to have someone to talk to and to share her pleasure in the game. The thought of going back to the apartment alone now was unappealing. She wasn't ready for the evening to end just yet.

Gideon's next words made her think that maybe he felt the same way, too.

"Why don't we all go out for a quick bite to eat?"

Lettie and Ethan shared a look. "Actually, we were planning on going back to the hospital after dropping Mallory off at the apartment," Ethan said.

"Then I'll tell you what: you two go on to the hospital, and I'll take Mallory to grab a burger somewhere and then drive her home—if that's okay with you," he said, looking questioningly at Mallory.

That was going too fast too soon. Spending time with him at a football game or in company with Lettie and Ethan was one thing—she wasn't ready to trust him with her life. "Oh, you don't have to do that—I'll just take a taxi or get a ride share or something. Really. I don't mind."

Secretly pleased that she hadn't leaped at his invitation, he replied, "I know I don't *have* to—I *want* to. I promise to deliver you safely to your door. Okay?"

She hesitated and glanced at Lettie. *Help!*

Understanding her cousin's silent plea, Lettie said, "We don't want to impose on you, Gideon."

Ethan, meanwhile, was getting a different message from Gideon. "I'm sure Gideon wouldn't have offered if it was an imposition."

"That's right!" Gideon agreed.

"I know you just met him, but I can vouch for him, Mallory," Ethan continued. "He really is a good guy. You'll be safe, I promise."

Mallory exchanged one last glance with Lettie before capitulating. "All right," she said, peering up at Gideon shyly. "Thank you."

"My pleasure," he said quietly although inwardly he was thinking *Yes!*

Lettie stepped forward and gave Mallory a quick hug. "Text me if you need me," she whispered. Then she and Ethan waved goodbye and walked off hand-in-hand.

Despite it being almost dusk, Gideon put on his sunglasses. Mallory followed suit with her own pair as they merged into the line of spectators moving slowly but steadily towards the exit. Gideon reached out and tucked her hand under his arm. "I don't want to lose you," he said with a grin.

She looked at her hand, feeling the hard curve of his biceps muscle, and then looked around at the crowd of people pressing around them. *Yes, better to have an arm to hold on to.* and gave a nod.

As they worked their way to the parking lot, cussing the game and reviewing some of the great p nessed. He enjoyed watching her face light up as she er recalled her favorite moments of the game.

Mallory, meanwhile, silently marveled at how comfortab with Gideon. This was the most at ease she had been with a man in a long time. *Is this how I used to be?*

"So where would you like to go?" he asked some time later as th sat in his modest Chevy Traverse and waited for a light to change. "Would you rather get something vegetarian?"

"No, a burger would be perfect."

Finally—a girl who's not afraid to eat. "Is it all right if we just get something from the drive-through? As you saw earlier, it gets crazy sometimes when people recognize me," he said ruefully, "so if you don't mind, we could just eat in the car."

With that came an idea so daring, Mallory felt almost breathless. She'd decided to trust him this much... should she take it a step further? She looked at him hesitantly as she steeled herself to make the offer. "I hope you don't take this the wrong way, but if you'd like—if you don't want to take the chance of being recognized—we could take the food back to my apartment to eat. But only if you want to," she added hastily, suddenly feeling that even Max would think she'd been *too* bold.

There was a pause as Gideon considered this. "Actually, Mallory, that sounds like a great idea." The light turned green, and as the SUV accelerated, he added with a grin, "If you want to know the truth, I was hoping you'd invite me in for a few minutes when I dropped you off, so this is even better! What burger places are near your apartment?"

She leaned back against her seat, relieved that he'd taken the invitation in the spirit intended.

...und as he followed Mallory into her ...onsole table, where Mallory placed ...mall foyer. To the right, a gray-up- ...ffee table and end tables, and two ...th navy blue cushions all looked ...abinet that held the flat-screen TV. ...ng table and the two pairs of mis- ...irift-store finds but, like the two bar ...en island, had been painted a bright ...cers flanked by filmy gray-and-white striped ...urned the windows and sliding door. Bright-colored ...n shades of navy, turquoise, yellow, and lime were nestled on ...ie sofa and chairs, and several abstract pictures in the same colors as the pillows brightened up the stark white walls.

"Wow, this is *way* better than any of Ethan's student apartments," he remarked, pausing to look at the signature on one of the paintings.

"Thanks," Mallory said, setting the bag of food on the island.

He brought the tray of drinks over. "I didn't know Lettie is an artist."

"She sure is—a very good one. She painted all of these."

"Nice. Do you paint, too?"

She chuckled and gestured to the console table, bar stools, and dining set. "Only furniture. Ethan's parents let us use their garage to paint them. My contribution to the décor was the pillows and the curtains. My sewing machine is one of the things I absolutely had to bring out here with me."

"So you made these? I'm impressed."

Her lips curved in a shy smile. "Stop. Shall we eat before everything gets cold?"

Minutes later, perched on the bar stools at the small kitchen island, they talked about themselves and their respective families as they ate their meal. In answer to Gideon's question, she told him her home was in a small town about 100 miles northeast of Albany. She briefly described her family and then explained how she'd come to L.A. to visit Lettie in January, had been impressed with the Pollard Institute, and decided to apply to the master's program.

Karen Lail

"I've officially been living here since the end of January and was fortunate enough to be able to start working part-time at Pollard's library in mid-February even though my classes didn't begin until June," she explained.

Mallory then changed the subject by asking him about *his* family and career. She knew his two older brothers were married, and Gideon told her with pride that he was now an uncle to two nephews and a niece. He went on to say that Gareth and his fiancée Rachel would be getting married the third Saturday in November. After their honeymoon, Gareth and Rachel would join the family in Branson, where the brothers were scheduled to perform nightly beginning the Friday after Thanksgiving through the second Thursday in December, and then they would all be home for the holidays. They were also getting ready to record yet another new album that would be released sometime in the new year.

"Oh, that's great," she said, watching him take a sip of his drink. "If you don't mind my asking, why the drums? I mean, did you all draw straws or something to decide which instrument each of you would play?"

He laughed. "No, we all started by playing piano, but as we got older, some of us decided to branch out. As a kid, Gabriel was always jumping and sliding around, playing air guitar, so no one was surprised when he wanted to learn electric guitar. As for me… for as long as I can remember, I've counted things: my footsteps, my heartbeats, the ticks of a clock, the taps of a hammer… anything. And I've always had a good feel for rhythm and syncopation." He smiled reminiscently. "As soon as I picked up my first set of drumsticks, I was hooked. But I like other percussion instruments, too. I think that's why, even now, our Christmas album is the one I personally am most proud of, because I was able to incorporate tubular bells and the jingle stick and the chime tree into so many of those songs."

It had been on the tip of her tongue to admit that "Christmas in the Key of G" was her favorite of all the Locke Brothers' songs; that seeing him sing it live in concert was one of her most cherished teenage memories. But she was afraid Gideon would write her off as just a sycophant, so instead she said, "There's nothing that says

Christmas more than bells and chimes."

Taking a French fry and dipping it in ketchup, Mallory missed Gideon's look of surprise.

That's funny—wasn't that exactly what Santa had said? He studied her for a moment when she raised her eyes back to his, and then smiled. *Just a coincidence.* "I couldn't agree more."

So engrossed were they in their conversation, they were both startled when the apartment door opened.

"Oh, hi," Lettie said, arching an inquisitive eyebrow at Mallory as she and Ethan came in.

"How's your grandma?" Gideon asked.

"She thinks there's 'too much fuss being made over a couple of bumps and bruises'—*her* words, not mine."

"That sounds like her," he grinned as he slid from the stool and started gathering up the food wrappers while Mallory carried their drink cups to the sink and dumped out the ice.

"Don't get up on our account," Lettie said, joining Mallory in the kitchen and pulling a package of microwave popcorn out of a cabinet. "We're just going to get a snack and watch TV. Want to join us?"

Gideon glanced at his watch. "No, I should probably go. Maybe another time."

"Okay. Good to see you, man," Ethan said as he and Gideon hugged.

"Likewise. Nice to meet you, Lettie."

"You, too, Gideon."

Mallory walked with him to the door as Lettie started the popcorn and Ethan pulled two cans of soda out of the refrigerator. Gideon held the door open, and Mallory stepped out into the hall with him, leaving the door slightly ajar.

"Mallory," he began. "Would it be all right if I called you sometime?"

With a sense of unreality, she heard herself answering, "Why, yes, I'd like that."

He pulled out his phone, went to his Contacts list, and typed in her name. "What's your number?"

"It's 518-555-3286."

He finished typing and showed her the screen to confirm the number. At her nod, he saved the entry and pocketed his phone.

"If you give me your phone, I'll add in my number. That way you'll see my caller ID," he offered.

"Okay." She stepped into the apartment, grabbed her phone from her purse, and handed it to him when she returned to the hallway.

He quickly typed in his information and passed the phone back to her.

"I'll call you in a couple of days," he promised as she stuffed the phone in one of her back pockets. "My schedule is pretty crazy until the middle of the week, but I'll call as soon as I get a chance."

"That's fine." They were silent a moment as they looked at each other, and then, holding out her right hand, Mallory said, "Thank you so much for dinner and for driving me home, Gideon."

Instead of shaking her hand, he grasped it with his left hand, and then took her other hand in his right, holding them both gently. "It was my pleasure. Thank *you* for keeping me company," he said with a grin. After another pause, he added, "I really enjoyed being with you today, Mallory."

"I enjoyed it, too." She drew her hands from his. "Good night."

"Talk to you soon."

But she wondered, as she closed the door behind her a moment later, if she was really ready for what might come.

CHAPTER 10

Wednesday, October 23rd

It was about 4:30 p.m. when Mallory walked into the apartment three days later and set down her laptop tote. "Oh, what a day," she remarked, sinking down on the sofa and hugging one of the pillows to her chest.

Lettie smiled sympathetically. "Maybe you'll have peace and quiet while Ethan and I are out tonight."

Mallory's phone rang. "Or not," she retorted, pulling it out and glancing at the caller ID. She set the pillow aside and straightened up. "Hi, Gideon," she said, surprised and, yes, pleased that he had actually called her.

"And that's my cue to leave," Lettie whispered with a smile, spinning on her heel and walking towards her bedroom.

Mallory and Gideon chatted for a few moments, and then he came to the point of his call. "Listen, we ended rehearsal early today, and I wanted to know if you'd like to have dinner with me? I know this is short notice, but I'd really like you to come—unless you have too much studying to do?"

She hesitated, fighting her long-standing habit of saying No. "I'd love to."

"Great! Do you like Italian? I thought we could try a new restaurant Graham told me about. It's a little upscale, but not stuffy."

"Yes, I love Italian."

"Good. Pick you up about 6:15?"

"I'll be ready."

"See you then."

Lettie walked back into the living room. "So… ?"

"He's taking me to dinner. Lettie, what does someone wear to a place that's 'a little upscale but not stuffy'?"

She smiled and pulled Mallory to her feet. "I know just the dress you should wear. It looks amazing on you."

She was ready about five minutes before Gideon had said to expect him, and by that time she was verging on panic. *Why, oh, why did I ever agree to go out with him? I can't do this—I just can't,* she told herself as she fiddled with the blue-and-white silk scarf Lettie had insisted on draping around her neck. But even as the thought crossed her mind, she reminded herself how comfortable she had felt with Gideon on Sunday. *Why should tonight be any different? Because there was no pressure on Saturday. Tonight is a date.*

Needing to compose herself, Mallory opened the sliding door, stepped out onto the balcony, and leaned against the railing as she tugged off the scarf. Absently winding the length of silk around her left hand, she looked out past the parking lot, watching as several windows in nearby homes and apartments lit up. Closing her eyes, she lifted her face to the breeze from the hot, dry Santa Ana winds blowing westward from the Nevada buttes and mountains, and listened to the twilight sounds of the city as she tried to clear her mind. And then her stomach lurched when she heard the doorbell ring. *Please, God, help me through this.* She stepped back inside, but Lettie was already heading to the door.

"Hi, Gideon," Mallory heard her say. Gideon murmured a response and then moved into Mallory's line of sight. He was strikingly handsome in a charcoal gray suit and a crisp white shirt with the top button undone. And, surprisingly, he wasn't wearing his wig tonight.

He immediately saw her amid the billowing curtains and smiled. "Hi, Mallory," he greeted, walking toward her. "You look *great,*" he said, taking in the marine blue, three-quarter-sleeved sheath dress that accentuated her slender build.

"Hi. You look nice, too," she managed to answer, futilely hoping he couldn't hear the quaver in her voice. She moved forward and reached for her purse and fine-knit cotton cardigan and then realized she still had the scarf wrapped around her hand. Hastily, she stuffed it into her purse.

"Are you ready to go?" he asked. When she didn't answer right away, Lettie looked at her tensely.

Gideon extended his hand, palm up.

As Mallory laid her palm on his and watched his fingers close around hers, that same sense of warm comfort she'd felt on Sunday filled her. *It's going to be all right.* She silently exhaled the breath she had been holding and looked up at him with a smile. "Yes, I'm ready."

Relieved, Lettie walked behind them as they headed to the door. "Have a good time, you two."

"Thanks," Gideon said, opening the door.

Mallory flashed a timid smile and passed in front of him out of the apartment.

He escorted her to an older-model silver Chevrolet Impala. "My car is being serviced so I'm driving this one tonight." He opened the passenger door for her. "It's a—"

"2013. The last year they made a six-passenger sedan, right?" Seeing his expression, she added, "My mom has one, too. She just can't bring herself to give it up."

"Same with us," he said, watching her with added interest as she slipped into the car.

The restaurant was quietly elegant, and the designer in her noted the architectural details appreciatively as the maître d' escorted Mallory and Gideon to a table near a window. Despite her best efforts to ignore the fact that this *was* a date—her first in over two years—and just concentrate on enjoying Gideon's company, his actions constantly reminded her of that very fact. Although he'd been well mannered on Sunday once they'd gotten past their prickly introduction, now he showed in so many subtle ways just how different was this night: taking her hand as they walked side-by-side, placing his hand at her waist to guide her around the smallest of obstacles, resting his hands on her shoulders for a moment as the maître d' pulled out her chair. Most of all, the earnest way he looked at her told Mallory that, for tonight at least, they were testing a new level in their acquaintance.

Three times during the meal, Gideon was approached by eager fans who wanted to get his autograph or to take a selfie with him. Mallory didn't mind the interruptions, since they gave her an opportunity to sit back and observe Gideon. Each time, a slight furrowing of the brow—as if he were worried—was the only sign that he was uncomfortable, but then he would smile and make small-talk with the girls while he signed his name or posed for a picture. The fans were oblivious to that fleeting expression of nervousness, but it reminded Mallory of the look she'd seen on his face when he was talking to the young women at the game.

"Sorry about that," Gideon said, resuming his seat after the third interruption.

"No need to apologize—I know it comes with the territory."

He cast a look around at the patrons nearest their table, noticing that some were snapping photos of them with their cell phones. "I was going to suggest we share a slice of cheesecake for dessert, but maybe we shouldn't. Posts have probably been popping up all over social media, saying that I've been seen here... which means we'll probably be confronted by paparazzi when we leave."

Mallory, who had been unaware of the interest of the other diners, looked up, alarmed, as she pushed her plate away. "Photographers?"

He nodded, concerned and puzzled by her panicked reaction. He saw her reach for her purse.

God, is she going to run out on me?

She suddenly stopped, her attention seemingly fixed on something inside her purse. Gideon watched in wonder as a mischievous smile replaced her look of panic.

She leaned forward and placed her hand on his arm. "I have an idea."

He bent closer to her. "I'm listening."

Gideon saw Mallory emerge from the ladies' room near the restaurant entrance. In the space of a few minutes, she had pulled her hair into a high ponytail, exchanged her contact lenses for a pair of dark-framed eyeglasses, covered the top half of her dress with her tightly buttoned sweater, and wrapped and knotted a scarf around her neck, the points draped jauntily over one shoulder. *She could pass for a flight attendant or cruise employee,* he marveled, pretending to take a sip of water as she exited the restaurant and handed the valet ticket to the attendant.

He smiled as the waiter came forward with the folder holding his credit card and the receipt. Swiftly he added a tip, calculated the total, and signed the merchant copy and, standing, tucked his copy and the credit card in his wallet. Then, ignoring the looks of admiration and the battery of cell phones aimed his way, he strolled towards the front, counting his steps silently.

He saw the Impala pull up under the portico. The attendant held the door open for Mallory; she handed him his tip, slid behind the wheel and continued to move across the seat towards the passenger side. Meanwhile, Gideon quickly pushed open the restaurant door and, as cameras flared belatedly, stepped into the car, closed the door, and put the car in gear. He and Mallory laughed gleefully as they sped out of the parking lot.

"That was great!" he chortled, snagging her hand and holding it as he steered with his left hand.

"It was like being in a spy novel!"

"I know, right? You were amazing! I can't believe you thought of that!"

"Design 101: accessories can change the look of a room—or a person," she answered with a smile as they stopped for a traffic light.

"I'm a believer. Thank you," he said, kissing the back of her hand as he looked at her.

"You're welcome," she answered breathlessly. "I'm sorry you didn't have a chance to get your dessert."

"Actually, I have an idea."

"Take-out?"

"Something even better."

"Oh, this is so good!" Mallory sighed, popping a spoonful of ice cream into her mouth.

Mouth full, Gideon could only nod his agreement.

"It's been *ages* since I've had a homemade sundae. Thank you for letting me crash your date," Garrison said. He was seated on the other side of Gideon at the kitchen island.

"I'm glad you could join us," Gideon replied.

Gideon had left his car parked in the driveway when he and Mallory arrived at the Locke house, and they had entered through the front door. He'd guided her through the foyer with its gracefully curved staircase, past the formal living room on the left, straight back to the large, open concept kitchen, dining area, and family room. Garrison had been seated at the island with his laptop and had invited them to join him. As she had taken her place on one of the stools, Mallory had noted the kitchen's finishes and layout of the kitchen with approval. The base cabinets and kitchen island were painted in a dark slate blue with white quartz countertops. The backsplash was a mosaic of rectangular pieces of slate of varying lengths, predominantly in the same shade of blue as the cabinets but with touches of ochre and tan and white, interspersed with brushed stainless tiles. The upper cabinets were a shade of off-white somewhere between bone and muslin, and the vent hood over the gas range was clad in mid-toned wood.

Garrison blotted his mouth with his napkin and stood up. "And now I'll leave the two of you in peace. It was very nice to meet you, Mallory."

"You too, Mr. Locke."

"Please, call me Garrison."

"'Night, Dad. I'll take care of the dishes," Gideon said, pushing away his empty bowl. He looked at Mallory. "Do you want to watch a movie?"

She glanced at the microwave clock. *After ten already?* "I would love to, Gideon, but I have an eight o'clock class tomorrow, so we should probably leave soon. Maybe another time?" she asked, stacking the empty bowls and standing up.

"Of course," he answered, rising from his stool.

Karen Lail

She carried the bowls and spoons to the sink. "I'll help you with the dishes before we go."

"I hope you had a good time tonight," Gideon remarked later as they reached the fourth floor of the apartment building and walked hand-in-hand down the hall.

"I had a *wonderful* time. I hope you did, too?"

"Absolutely—especially seeing your Super Designer Woman act…"

She shook her head deprecatingly. "It was nothing."

"But from now on," he continued, "maybe we should only go to restaurants that have a drive-through. Or… by any chance, are you free on Tuesday?"

"I'm working at the library that morning, but I'll be off at eleven-thirty," she answered as she unlocked the door.

He held the door open and followed her inside. "Would you like to go on a picnic?"

"Oh, that sounds like fun!"

"I think so, too. Why don't I pick you up at, say, twelve-fifteen? Will that give you enough time to get back from campus and get ready?"

"Yes, that should be fine."

"Or, if you prefer, I can pick you up from the library as soon as you get off work. I'll be driving past the institute anyway to get to your place."

"I'd still have to come back to the apartment to change."

"Not a problem. And if Gareth and Rachel don't have other plans, would it be all right if we double-dated?"

"Of course. How about if *I* get the food so it doesn't have to be in the cooler so long?"

"All right, but I'm paying for everything."

She smiled saucily at him. "We'll see." They quickly agreed on a menu.

"I'll see you Tuesday, then." Tentatively, he put his hands on her waist, took a step closer, and then halted. He stood looking at her for a long moment, his eyes seeming to ask a question.

She dipped her head shyly and then rested her hands on his shoulders and lifted her face. At the last minute, though, she turned her head and Gideon's lips landed on her right cheek.

"Sorry," she said self-consciously as he drew back. "I just… what I mean is—"

"It's too soon. I understand."

She nodded gratefully.

He cradled the left side of her face with one hand. "I'll call or text you tomorrow, all right?"

"Okay."

He drew his fingers down her cheek, briefly cupping her chin before lowering his hand. "Goodnight, Mallory."

"Goodnight."

He waited while she stepped inside the apartment and softly closed the door. Then, smiling slightly, he turned and headed back to the elevator.

"Mallory seems like a nice girl," Garrison observed when Gideon entered the kitchen.

Gideon pulled a glass out of a cabinet. "She is," he answered, reaching into the refrigerator for the pitcher of filtered water.

Garrison turned a page of his magazine as Gideon filled his glass. "Do you plan to see her again soon?"

"On Tuesday," he said, placing the pitcher back in the refrigerator and closing the door. "Why?" he asked, joining his father at the kitchen island.

Garrison closed his magazine and took off his reading glasses. "I'm glad you're dating again, son."

"But—?" He took a sip of water, his eyes fixed on his father.

"Just take your time and get to know each other."

A smile played around Gideon's mouth. "Trust me, Dad… we're taking it slow."

Karen Lail

CHAPTER 11

Tuesday, October 29ᵗʰ

"Sorry to be so slow," the student apologized as he rested one crutch against the circulation desk and, balancing with the other crutch, started pulling books out from under his arm one at a time and laying them on the desk surface.

"Not a problem. It must be hard to manage everything with that broken leg," Mallory remarked as she dragged each book toward her, her bracelet softly clinking.

"Yes, it's been a challenge," he admitted, placing the last book on the desk. He lifted his lanyard from his neck and passed it to her. "That's the last time I try to water ski."

Wincing in sympathy, Mallory scanned the attached ID and handed it back to him. He draped the lanyard around his neck again as she quickly scanned and stacked the books to one side of her.

"These are all due on November nineteenth," she stated, tearing the receipt from the printer and inserting it in one of the books and pushing the stack forward.

"Thanks," he said, beginning to reach for the books.

"If you'd like, I'll put them in your backpack for you."

"Would you please? That would be great."

She smiled. "Just stay there. I'll come around to you." As she moved out from behind the desk, she noticed Gideon observing her from a few feet away, a smile hovering on his lips.

She stilled for a moment and then held up a finger, and he gave an answering nod.

She really is a kind person, he thought, following her movements as she slipped the books into the student's backpack and then passed the other crutch to him.

"Thanks," the student said, positioning the crutch under his arm.

"My pleasure," Mallory answered.

Gideon moved forward as the student loped slowly away. "Now I understand why you said you need to change. Since this is a college library, I somehow just assumed you would be wearing jeans."

Mallory cast a quick glance down at her black-and-white geometric print blouse and black dress pants. "I guess dressing professionally is something that was engrained in me from working at my parents' clinic."

"You look nice. I hope you don't mind being seen with me like this," he teased.

Her gaze skimmed over his dark blue Henley shirt, faded jeans, and comfortable tennis shoes. "Well, I'll make an exception just this once."

"Thank you, m'lady," he said with a mock bow and a grin. "Are you ready? Gareth and Rachel are waiting for us in the car."

She glanced over her shoulder and spied a girl approaching, a cash drawer held in her hands. Mallory turned back to Gideon. "Yes, that's my relief. I just need to turn in my cash drawer and sign out. In the meantime," she said, going around the desk and leaning down to pull out a couple of books, "would you hold these for me, please?"

"I'll be glad to." He picked up the books and tucked them between his left arm and hip.

And suddenly he felt like he fit in.

───────────────────────

Mallory was immediately drawn to Gareth and Rachel and they in turn were disposed to like her at first for Gideon's sake but, the more they talked to her, on her own merit. After reaching Mallory's apartment building, they volunteered to help Gideon pack up the cooler while Mallory changed clothes, so all four of them rode up the elevator to Mallory's apartment. In the kitchen, Mallory slipped off her bracelet and placed it on the kitchen island with her purse and then, opening the refrigerator, quickly pointed out all the food containers to be packed. As she scurried towards her bedroom, the bracelet caught Gideon's eye; he picked it up and read the engraving. Pensively he set it gently back in place and then turned to help his brother and Rachel.

It was just after one o'clock when they arrived at the Pacific Palisades location that Gideon and Gareth had chosen for the picnic. As the two couples gathered around the open hatch of Gareth's black SUV, Mallory breathed in the crisp scent of pine tinged with salt spray. Her eyes fluttered closed for a moment. *I need this.* She smiled up at Gideon as she took the tote bag of tableware from him.

"What a great place for a picnic," she said.

"Yeah, we haven't been here in a long time," he agreed, pulling out the cooler of food while Gareth and Rachel each grabbed a handle and lifted a second cooler from the hatch.

"Here, let me help," Mallory said, reaching for a handle with her free hand.

Because it was a school day, the park was fairly empty, but Rachel still insisted on scouting out the most secluded picnic table they could find. She and Gareth covered the table with a vinyl tablecloth and set out the drinks, ice, condiments, and tableware while Gideon and Mallory unpacked the food: deli meats, lettuce, tomato slices, provolone and American cheese, pickles, potato salad, and brownies.

"Wow, what a spread! This is awesome, guys," Gareth said appreciatively as he scooped potato salad onto his plate.

"Hey, go easy on that," Gideon warned. "You have a tux you need to fit into in a couple of weeks."

"You're right," Gareth agreed and then mischievously added another spoonful to his plate.

Somehow Mallory made it through that meal. Between Gareth's mangled jokes, Rachel and Gareth's lighthearted teasing, and Gideon and Gareth's amusing stories of their childhood and life on tour, it was all she could do to eat. She couldn't remember laughing as hard or as much since coming to L.A.

After lunch, Gareth produced a football from the bottom of the tote bag. "Who wants to do some passing?" he asked, tossing the ball from hand to hand.

"I will," Gideon replied, standing up.

"You two have fun. I'm going to just sit here and enjoy the sunshine," Rachel said, closing her eyes and tipping her face skyward.

Gareth tossed the football to Gideon before turning to his fiancée. "Oh, no you don't," he smiled, pulling Rachel to her feet. "You can enjoy the sunshine while we pass the ball." He looked at each of them. "So what do you say? Guys against the gals? Oh, and Mallory, don't let that prim demeanor fool you. Rachel's a tomboy at heart."

"Then that makes two of us," Mallory replied, snatching the football from Gideon, handing it off to Rachel, and running about ten yards before turning, holding out her arms and waggling her fingers. Rachel threw the ball and Mallory caught it easily. She immediately shot it back to Rachel, who caught it and spun around.

"We are such toast," Gareth remarked to his brother.

"*Yeah,* we are." They shrugged and ran out to join the girls.

———————

"I haven't done that in a long time," Mallory said breathlessly, handing the football to Gideon as they came back to the picnic table. Behind them, Rachel and Gareth were having a quiet conversation as they eyed Mallory and Gideon. After a moment, they joined them at the table.

"We're going to check out the overlook," Gareth said, leaning over to snatch up the last brownie. "Want to come?"

"You go ahead," Gideon answered, his eyes fixed on Mallory.

Mallory watched the couple head up the trail and then looked back at Gideon. Their eyes locked. Troubled by his unreadable expression, she sprang up and began putting the food containers back in the cooler, glancing at him from time to time. Her mind skimmed over the events of the afternoon. *Did I say or do something wrong? What is he thinking? Why is he looking at me so strangely?* She concentrated on lowering and fastening the lid as she fought the swell of panic rising in her.

Then Gideon's hand covered hers and, after a beat, she ventured a peek at him.

"Shall we join Gareth and Rachel?" he suggested.

"Okay."

They hadn't gone very far when they spotted a playground.

Mallory and Gideon traded looks. This time, there was no question about what Gideon was thinking.

Mallory broke away from him. "I'll race you!" she called over her shoulder as she ran towards the swing-set where a pair of adult swings hung idly side by side.

Gideon chuckled and dashed after her, soon catching up. They each grabbed a swing and launched themselves.

Mallory delighted in the effort of swinging back and forth, higher and still higher, until it seemed she could touch the treetops. After a few minutes, Gideon laughingly called a halt to the "race" and they slowed to a dawdling pace that enabled them to talk. His mood was suddenly quiet, subdued, his features settling into the same disconcerting expression as before. Mallory waited, torn between curiosity about what was on his mind, dread that he was about to end their relationship before it had really begun, and vexation for allowing herself to become so vulnerable so quickly.

She breathed an inward prayer for fortitude.

"You've been hurt a lot in the past, haven't you?" Gideon said, more as a statement of fact than a question.

She looked at him in surprise and dismay. "Did Lettie say something to you?"

"No, not a word. But from the time we met I can *feel* it. I know you like me, but now and then you get scared or lose confidence—like the other night before we went out, right?" he said, and she nodded. "But look at you: You're beautiful, and intelligent, and fun to be with—on the surface, you seem like one of the *last* people who'd feel insecure. The only thing that accounts for it, that makes *any* sense at all, is that you've been hurt somewhere along the line."

"Yes," she admitted.

"But it goes beyond being hurt, doesn't it?" he persisted. When she didn't respond, he said gently, "I read the engraving on your bracelet."

Her hand instinctively touched the wrist where she typically wore the bangle.

Stopping his swing, he reached out and took her hand. "Would you tell me about it?"

Mallory sighed. *He deserves to know.* So, quietly, baldly, she told him how she'd stayed at the library later than she'd intended one night just weeks before the end of her senior year of college in Albany, New York. How she'd been too absorbed in mentally organizing her research paper to be aware of her surroundings as she walked back to her dorm. Being grabbed and knocked to the ground, and the desperate struggle that followed. The two couples who'd happened to leave the library just minutes behind her, and whose timely intervention had scared off the assailant. The arrival of campus security, two of the officers transporting her to the infirmary while the others examined the scene and took witness statements. The questioning by the security officers at the infirmary and the pictures... the endless pictures... they took of every bruise and scrape and tear.

She broke off with a barely repressed shudder.

No wonder she was upset about the photographers the other night. Gideon's mind flooded with questions but he merely squeezed her hand gently and waited.

After a pause, she continued on, describing her retreat back home as soon as the semester was over, not even staying for her graduation ceremony. The lingering feelings of humiliation and fear, and all she had done to try to cope, cutting herself off from everyone except her loved ones; limiting her life to home and church and the eye clinic; making herself as plain and colorless and unnoticeable as possible... Her mother's diagnosis of cancer and subsequent surgery and treatment. And then the final blow: her fiancé of just six months breaking off their engagement, unable or unwilling to accept the changes in her.

Gideon felt a flash of anger. *What a jerk.*

She went on, describing how Max had suddenly moved back home the September after the attack, putting his life on hold for her, supporting her, encouraging her, stretching her as no therapist could. With him beside her, she had ventured further and further outside the rigid home-church-clinic triangle she'd drawn around her life, going to the grocery store, the hair salon, the mall... until by the following spring she was confident enough to run errands alone. The greatest gift he gave her, though, was making her laugh again.

"It sounds like you two are really close," Gideon remarked.

"Oh, we are. I guess it's a twin thing."

"And he's the one who encouraged you to move out here?"

"Well, not right away. My parents had been trying to get me to pursue my master's degree, but I didn't want to go back to my old school. And then right before Christmas last year, I had a strange encounter with someone—it's hard to explain, but… Well, maybe I'll tell you about that some other time. The point is, between meeting that person and then coming out to visit Lettie this past January, I knew it was time to try to open up again, to get back on track. But it's been hard. I really have to fight myself sometimes." She paused, wanting desperately to make him understand, but uncertain how. And then she spied the row of spring-mounted rocking animals a short distance away. "I guess you could say I've been sort of like a turtle," she said, pointing to the rocking figure. "As soon as something spooks me—something that somebody says or does, or something *I* say or do that makes me feel exposed in some way—I pull back tight into my shell and I'll stay hidden until whoever it is just gives up and goes away. It's cowardly, I know, but I found it's easier to withdraw than risk being hurt."

A turtle. Yes, exactly, he thought, but he merely replied, "There's nothing cowardly about wanting to protect yourself." *I wish I could do more of that myself sometimes.*

"Maybe not, as long as it doesn't keep you from God's purpose for your life. That's what I am still struggling with—finding that balance, you know?" She hesitated a moment before adding, "I hope you can be patient with me."

He drifted his swing close to hers and cupped the side of her face, his thumb lightly stroking her cheekbone. "Someone reminded me—also just before Christmas, coincidentally—that good things are worth waiting for."

She looked at him, struck, as she treasured up the gift of those words.

"Thank you for trusting me enough to tell me. I know it was hard for you," he said softly. "And I didn't mean to bring back bad memories for you. I can't imagine going through all of that."

"You needed to know. And as for my ex-fiancé, well, I've long since realized *that* relationship was never meant to be."

"No, apparently not," Gideon agreed quietly. "If it's any consolation, though, I've had to tell myself the very same thing more than once."

She considered his words. "It must be hard for you, not knowing whether a girl likes you for *you*, or because of who you are—one of the famous Locke Brothers."

He nodded and looked off into the distance. "My parents protected us as much as they could, but it's something we've *all* had to deal with at one time or another." He looked again at her. "To be honest, I've had my own issues with trusting people."

Held by his gaze, Mallory felt compelled to say, "I hope you know you can trust me."

"Oh, yes," he answered as he gathered her to him, swing and all, and held her for a moment. He drew back slightly, his forehead resting against hers as he looked into her eyes.

"There you are," Gareth said as he and Rachel joined them at the swing-set.

Rachel laid a restraining hand on Gareth's arm. "Sorry—we didn't mean to intrude."

Gideon and Mallory stood up and released their swings. "No, it's fine," he said, glancing at Mallory with a smile as he laced his fingers with hers.

"I guess we should be heading back," Gareth said apologetically. "We're going to be cutting it close."

"Gareth and Rachel are meeting with the organist this evening to finalize all the music," Gideon explained to Mallory.

"Oh, nice."

Rachel and Gareth exchanged a look, and then Rachel went over and took hold of Mallory's arm. "Come on, Mallory. Let's go ahead and start packing up everything."

"Sounds good."

"What was that all about?" Gideon asked when the girls were out of earshot.

"It's about Mallory. Rachel and I talked about it, and we agree." Gideon waited for the verdict.

"So how did you and Gareth meet?"

Rachel laughed. "You know that saying: 'I knew him when…'? Well, I literally *did*. We met in second grade, and we were in the same class each year until sixth grade, when Gareth and his brothers started singing professionally. Their parents hired a tutor for the boys since they were touring so much, so Gareth left our school and we lost touch with each other. We reconnected about three years ago at a charity event that my parents were coordinating."

"That's right… Gideon said your family has an event planning business."

She nodded. "One of our servers cut her hand on a broken glass and needed to get some stitches, so I was filling in for her. I was circulating with a tray of hors d' oeuvres and ended up in front of Gareth. Of course *I* knew who *he* was, but surprisingly he recognized me too, even after all those years. He wanted to chat with me, but I told him I couldn't since I was on duty, so he asked for my phone number. He called me the next day to ask me out on a date." Rachel paused as she and Mallory reached the picnic table. "About ten days later, they left for a tour in Europe but we texted each other when we could. Then his mom died unexpectedly, and of course the whole family pretty much holed up after that. But I would bring over a meal to Gareth, Gideon, and their dad every week or so, just to check in on them. And, finally, he was ready to pick our relationship back up. Now here we are, just a little over three weeks away from our wedding." She looked around and then drew her phone out of her back pocket. "Want a sneak peek at the bridesmaid dress?"

"I'd love it!" she answered, moving closer to Rachel. Rachel scrolled to a picture and held up the phone. "Oh, my gosh—this dress is almost *exactly* like the one I had picked out for *my* bridesmaids—same inverted pleats, same lace bodice and sweetheart neckline, just a different color."

Rachel swiveled her head to glance at Mallory. "Wait… what? You mean you were *married*?"

Mallory laughed self-consciously. "No, I was engaged a couple of years ago."

"Really? What happened? Or would you rather not talk about it?"

She hesitated. "Let's just say he wasn't ready for the vow of 'For better or for worse.'"

"Then it's a good thing you found out when you did," Rachel said decisively.

"Yes, I realize that… *now*. So what colors did you choose for the flowers?"

She scrolled to another picture that was a montage of pale lavender and champagne colored roses, mauve-pink peonies, seeded eucalyptus, lotus pods, and copper-dipped gingko leaves. "The bouquets will be tied with plum-colored ribbon to match the bridesmaid dresses." She pointed to the champagne roses. "This is the color of my mom's dress."

"Rachel, your flowers are going to be stunning."

"Thanks." She pocketed her phone and followed Mallory to the table. The girls were quiet for a moment as they cleared off the picnic table. "So is Gideon the first guy you've gone out with since your engagement ended?" Rachel asked as she and Mallory folded the tablecloth.

"As a matter of fact, he is."

"What do the folks back home think about you dating one of the Locke Brothers?"

"Well, I haven't exactly told them."

"What?"

"I mean, I told them I had a dinner date with a guy named Gideon, but I didn't tell them it was Gideon *Locke*."

"Why not?"

Mallory shrugged. "I guess because—it just seems so unreal, you know? Me, a small-town New England girl, going on a date with someone famous? I like him a lot, but technically this is only our second date. Telling them just seems… I don't know… premature,

Karen Lail

even boastful. So I thought it was best to just keep it private for now."

"I can understand that. But as someone who is about to marry into the family, let me tell you: Sooner or later, the media are going to track down who you are, and your picture will be splashed all over the tabloids and TV. So don't wait to tell your family. They need to hear it from you first, *before* reporters and photographers start haunting your home town."

"Oh."

"You okay?" Gideon asked, coming up beside her.

She mustered a smile. "Yes, I'm fine," she said, reaching down for one of the handles of the food cooler.

Gideon got out of the car with Mallory.

"Oh, you don't need to walk me up. I know you're all in a hurry," she protested as he walked around the back of the SUV to retrieve the cooler.

"We've got time," Rachel said.

"Okay. Bye, Rachel. Bye, Gareth. I enjoyed meeting you," she said as Gideon came up beside her.

"You, too, Mallory."

"Be back in a minute," Gideon said to Rachel and Gareth, nudging the door closed with his elbow.

Gideon set the picnic cooler down as he and Mallory stopped outside the apartment door. He clasped his arms around her and she placed a hand against his chest. "I had a great time with you today," he said.

"I did too."

"So I have two questions for you: Will you have dinner with my family and me Saturday night? The whole family is getting together for a cookout."

"Yes, I'd like that."

"And the second question: Will you be my date for Rachel and Gareth's wedding?"

Mallory sat on her bed and stared at the Face Time contact list on her phone. Sighing, she pressed the button next to a name. After a moment, Meredythe's face appeared on the screen. "Hi, Mom. You're still at the clinic?" Mallory glanced at her bedside clock. Six-thirty Eastern Time.

"Yes. Your dad, Aidan, and I were just going over some final things for the day, and then we're taking Max to dinner before he heads back to campus."

At that moment, her father and brothers stepped into the background and called greetings to her.

"Oh, wow, so you're *all* there," she said, smiling weakly. "Hi, guys!"

"Is everything all right?" Roger asked.

"Yes, I'm fine. There's just something you need to know." And then she hesitated, struggling with her conviction that it was too soon to be having this conversation with her family.

"Out with it, sis," Max said. "What's going on?"

"Mom, remember me telling you about my date with Gideon?"

"Yes, of course."

"Well, what I *didn't* tell you is that he's Gideon Locke."

"As in the Locke Brothers?" Aidan asked, amazed.

"Yes. I didn't say anything before because… well—"

"You didn't know what would come of it," her mom finished. Mallory nodded.

"Have you seen him since then?"

"Yes, today as a matter of fact. We went on a picnic with his brother Gareth, and Gareth's fiancée, Rachel. Rachel is the one who said I should tell you, in case the media finds out."

As the conversation between Mallory and her parents and Aidan continued, Max surreptitiously took out his phone, looked up Gideon's name, and with deepening concern began reading.

CHAPTER 12

Wednesday, October 30th

Gideon rose from the children's table where his nephews, Jesse and David, were busily cutting out pumpkin shapes, and pressed his phone to his ear. "Hi, Kendra."

"Where are you?" Kendra asked, hearing the strains of "Baby Shark" in the background.

"I'm babysitting while Gabriel and Courtney have a lunch date," he answered, stepping out into the hallway and partially closing the door to the boys' room. "What's up?"

"I wanted to see what you've decided about tonight's party."

"I don't know, Kendra. If one of the others was going, too, it would be a no-brainer, but I don't want to be the only one representing the Locke Brothers."

"You know it would be good publicity if you go."

"Yes, I know. But I hate these things."

"It's all part of the job."

He paused a moment. "I don't have a date."

"That's okay—there will plenty of others there who are flying solo."

Gideon sighed and rolled his eyes heavenward. "Okay, fine. I'll go. But only for twenty minutes."

"An hour."

"Forty minutes and no more."

"All right—forty minutes. I'll send a town car to pick you up at, say, seven-thirty?"

"I can drive myself."

"Gideon," Kendra began, frustration evident in her voice.

"Okay, okay—a town car it is." At that moment, a high-pitched cry came from the boys' room. "Uh-oh, gotta go." Gideon burst into the room and looked from Jesse's anguished face to David's remorseful one. "What happened?"

Jesse pointed tragically.

"It is now two-fifty-nine p.m. Wednesday. Your projects are due by five p.m. on Friday," the professor cautioned. "See me *now* if you have any concerns."

The girl next to Mallory grimaced as they rose from their seats. "I think he's talking to me. What about you? Will you be done by Friday?"

"I should be. My plan is to finish the model this evening. That should leave me plenty of time before Friday to put the final touches on it."

"Lucky you. Oh, I'd better hurry before Dr. Ames leaves. See you on Friday."

"Good luck!"

"Thanks," the girl said, rushing towards the front of the classroom.

Mallory's phone pinged as she zipped and shouldered her laptop tote.

SOS!!! Please call ASAP!

Lagging after her classmates into the hallway, she pressed the call button and held the phone to her ear. "I got your message. What's wrong?... You're where?... Yes, I can be there in five minutes."

Mallory looked around as she approached the library parking lot, but saw no signs of Gideon's car. Startled, she spun around and drew back in alarm when a mini-van pulled up alongside her and the side door closest to her slid open.

"It's okay—it's just me," Gideon said. "Get into the front seat and I'll introduce you."

As the side door closed, Mallory climbed into the front passenger seat and turned slightly to look at the other occupants of the van.

"Mallory, this is my sister-in-law Courtney—Gabriel's wife. And this," he said, fondly laying a hand on the head of the small boy

Karen Lail

beside him, "is their oldest son, Jesse."

Mallory exchanged greetings with them, noting as she did so the signs of recent tear stains on Jesse's cheeks, his hands plucking fretfully at the straps of his car seat.

"We have a crisis," Gideon stated, "and it's my fault."

"Gideon left the room while Jesse and David were cutting with scissors," Courtney explained, reaching for a tote bag that rested on the center console.

"Oh? *Oh!*" Mallory exclaimed when Courtney held up several cut pieces of what had once been a two-piece Megawatt Commando superhero costume, the cut edges jagged and frayed.

"We were playing Baby Shark," Jesse said, his face puckering as two fresh tears oozed from his eyes.

"And David apparently pretended the scissors were shark jaws," Gideon finished.

"May I see?" Mallory asked. Courtney passed over the pieces one at a time: a leg that had been cut off mid-thigh, another leg that had been cut off just above the mock boot top, the remainder of the pants and attached utility belt, and then the top of the costume, which had a small slash in one sleeve but was otherwise intact. Mallory looked at the small boy again. "You like the Megawatt Commandos, Jesse?"

He sniffed dolefully and nodded.

"So does my niece Cassidy."

"Jesse had his heart set on being a Megawatt Commando for Halloween," Gideon said. "We've been to three stores, looking for a new costume, but they're all sold out of it."

"I can sew on buttons and mend a seam or a hem, but *this*… This is *way* past my skill level," Courtney said helplessly.

"So I told Courtney that, since you sew, maybe you would be able to salvage this for us?" Gideon asked.

"But only if you have time," Courtney interjected hastily. "If you can't do it, we'll just have to come up with another plan."

Mallory hesitated, glancing down at her laptop tote and then shifting her gaze back to Courtney, to Gideon, and finally resting on Jesse's hopeful little face. *I will just have to work extra hard and long on my project tomorrow night.* She held up the top of the costume. "Jesse, the only way I can fix this sleeve is if I sew another lightning bolt on it. Is that okay?"

"You mean I'll have an *extra* lightning patch?" he asked excitedly.

She smiled at him. "Yes, just like the commando leader."

"Yay!"

"What about the pants?" Gideon asked quietly.

"There's no way to repair them, so I'll have to get some fabric that matches as closely as possible and make a new pair. But I'll be able to reuse the boot tops and utility belt."

Courtney broke into a relieved smile. "Oh, thank you so much!"

"My pleasure."

"And we'll help you however we can. We're not going to just leave this all to you, are we, Court?"

"Oh, not at all. Just show me what to do."

"Okay." She smiled again at Jesse. "Let's go fix your costume!"

"Yay!" Jesse repeated.

Following a quick trip to a fabric store, they headed to Mallory's apartment, arriving just behind Ethan.

Oh, that's right—it's their one-year anniversary, Gideon thought, taking in Ethan's dress shirt and pants as he moved to greet his friend. Pulling back from their man-hug, he gave Ethan's shoulder a squeeze. Ethan bobbed his chin and smiled.

On hearing about the costume disaster, Lettie looked at Ethan. "Do we have time to help?"

"Sure," he replied.

Settling the folds of her dress around her as she perched on a stool, Lettie invited Jesse to sit at the kitchen island with her while she drew a pattern for the lightning bolt appliqué. Meanwhile, Gideon and Mallory grabbed the sewing machine and sewing basket from Mallory's room and carried them to the dining table. Opening the basket, Mallory picked up a seam ripper and demonstrated to Gideon and Courtney how to slice through the threads.

"We'll remove the pant pieces from the boot tops and utility belt, and then I'll use the pieces as a template to cut out and sew the new pair of pants," she explained, handing the seam ripper to Gideon and a second one to Courtney.

"And then we just reattach the utility belt and the boot tops," Courtney finished excitedly.

"That's right."

Gideon looked at his sister-in-law. "Why don't you do the boot tops and I'll handle the utility belt?"

"Sounds like a plan."

"I think we need some music for all of this," Ethan announced, reaching for his phone.

The atmosphere was festive as they all worked on their various tasks. While Courtney and Gideon ripped apart seams, Mallory sewed "fishbone" stitches to close the gash in the sleeve, and Lettie and Ethan took turns guiding Jesse's hand as he painstakingly cut the lightning bolt from a swatch of silver satin. When they had all completed their respective assignments, Mallory set up the ironing board and showed Courtney how to fuse and then whip-stitch the lightning bolt to the sleeve. Next, she and Gideon spread out the length of bright red satin they had purchased and pinned the pant pieces to it. Gideon carefully cut out the new pant pieces and Mallory threaded her sewing machine and filled a bobbin. Meanwhile, Lettie, Ethan, and Jesse alternately danced and showed off their Megawatt Commando moves. As Mallory started sewing up the pants, Gideon and Courtney whirled over to join the others. Mallory paused to watch their antics and, chuckling, turned her attention back to the sewing machine. Before she could resume stitching, however, Gideon sprinted back over to her, grabbed her hand, and drew her into the joyful impromptu dance party.

"All done," Lettie sang out as she set down the iron and held up both parts of the costume before passing them one at a time to Courtney.

Mallory looked from the costume to Jesse. "What do you think?" she asked.

"It's awesome!" Jesse cried. "Thank you!"

"You're welcome."

Gideon watched as Courtney finished folding the top loosely. "It's hard to believe that just a few hours ago, we thought we'd have to trash the costume."

Courtney placed the top and pants in her bag and engulfed Mallory in a grateful hug. "You're such a lifesaver! Thank you so much for everything!"

"I was happy to help, but it took all of us to get it done so quickly. We make a great team," Mallory said, smiling at each one in turn.

Ethan grinned as he slipped his arm around Lettie's waist. "I'll say. I don't know about the rest of you, but I've never been to a sewing dance party before. It was a blast."

Mallory briefly lifted her gaze to Gideon's. "Yes it was."

Ethan glanced at the microwave clock. "Uh-oh, we'd better go so we don't lose our dinner reservation," he prompted Lettie, urging her towards the door.

"Okay. See you later, everyone," Lettie called over her shoulder amid cries of goodbye and thanks.

Ethan's eyes met Gideon's one last time. Gideon gave a nod, and Ethan smiled before following Lettie.

"We'd better go, too," Courtney remarked.

Jesse tipped his face up towards his mother. "Can I wear the costume home, Mommy? Please?"

"No, I think we'd better keep this out of reach until it's time to go trick-or-treating tomorrow night," she answered gently.

"Awww," he replied, disappointed.

She handed the tote bag to her son. "But you can carry it to the car."

"Okay."

"Cheer up, buddy. Tomorrow will be here before you know it," Gideon assured him.

Courtney beamed at Mallory. "Thank you again, Mallory. I guess we'll see you on Saturday?"

"Yes, I'm looking forward to it," she replied.

"I'll catch up with you in a minute," Gideon told his sister-in-law.

She nodded and pulled the door closed as she and Jesse stepped out into the hall.

Gideon turned back to Mallory. "Listen, there's something you need to know: I'm going to a party tonight. It's one of those show business things that's more work than pleasure, where everyone comes to be seen and photographed—and maybe have a chance to talk about their latest project to one of the reporters. I would have asked you to go with me, but frankly I was hoping I could get out of it. But unfortunately Kendra told me I have to go. Anyway, I just wanted you to know so you're not surprised if you see or hear anything on the news."

"I understand." But, for a fleeting moment, she felt a little hurt that he hadn't at least invited her—even while she shrank from the thought of facing a throng of photographers and celebrities. "It would have been hard for me to go anyway, since I have a project due on Friday."

"Oh, I'm sorry—I didn't know we were keeping you from working on something."

"No, it's fine—really. I have more than enough time to finish it. Besides, who else could have saved you from such a rookie mistake?" she teased.

He laughed. "Only you. Thank you so much—for everything."

"My pleasure."

He leaned in to kiss her cheek. "Goodnight, Mallory. I'll see you on Saturday."

The party was held at the newly constructed home of one of Hollywood's most courted couples, music producer Dirk Stevens and his wife, actress Kate Kirkland. This was the first gathering at their new home, but Dirk and Kate's invitation had made it clear it was neither a housewarming nor, despite the fact that the next day was Halloween, a costume party. As he stepped out of the town car, Gideon scanned the exterior. The house was laid out like a very wide capital H. A courtyard of tumbled pavers, potted shrubs, and what appeared to be a sculpted marble fountain fronted the house. While the house looked attractive enough from the outside, once Gideon passed through the double front doors, he wished Mallory were with him. The central section of the house boasted an imposing twenty-foot high foyer, a colonnaded hallway that spanned the width of the house, and a sunken great room with an appalling number of intricately carved pillars, arches, and wall niches. Some were artfully chipped; others had fine cracks to make it appear as though they had been found in an architectural dig and carefully pieced back together. He could see part of a dining room and a billiard room in one wing; he assumed the other wing contained the private quarters of the couple and their three children. The collapsible glass wall of the great room had been opened fully, revealing a large patio with assorted dining tables and lounge areas, an Olympic-size pool with a swim-up bar, and a fire pit.

How she would laugh at this.

Gideon shook hands with Dirk Stevens, the moment captured for posterity by a photographer. Misinterpreting the look on Gideon's face, Dirk breezily waved a wine glass. "Kate was so enchanted by some of the Roman ruins we saw while we were filming in Italy two years ago that she insisted we include some of those features in our new home."

"I've never seen anything like it," Gideon managed to say with a straight face. "Where *is* Kate, by the way?"

"Oh, she's giving some of our guests a tour of the house. The next tour will be starting in a few minutes, if you care to join it. In the meantime, you'll find refreshments down the steps and to the right."

"Thanks."

He walked determinedly under the arch that spanned the three steps leading down to the great room, the pulsating music providing the cadence for his steps as he crossed to the bar. "Ginger ale, please." As the bartender selected a highball glass and poured the beverage, Gideon's fingers drummed on the bar top. *One thing about Dirk and Kate's parties: the music was invariably good.*

Placing a tip in the snifter glass marked for that purpose, he accepted the glass with thanks. Turning, Gideon pasted on his camera smile and ventured into the noisy, glittering crowd. Fortunately, most of the people were known to him. Some of them he had worked with on music videos in the past; a few he genuinely liked. Dutifully, he moved from group to group, greeting the partygoers, listening politely to the conversation, and adding occasional comments of his own, always keeping his features rigorously schooled and his actions restrained. Painful experience had taught him that photographers delighted in capturing awkward or suggestive moments.

Guests continued to arrive, and the music volume increased as the voice level rose. Dirk and Kate left their position by the front door and smilingly descended the steps to join their guests. Gideon returned to the bar for a fresh ginger ale. Holding his highball glass up and away from his body, he eased through the press of laughing, talking, and posturing celebrities and at last emerged into the comparative quiet of the patio. He set his glass on a nearby table and looked at his watch.

Ten minutes to go.

Reclaiming his glass, he nodded to one of the other guests who had sought a few minutes' peace out here. In the background beyond Gideon's field of vision, a photographer snapped a couple of rapid-fire shots. Sipping his drink, Gideon strolled around the pool deck to the fire pit. He paused, the flames casting a dancing glow on his face.

"Gideon?" a female voice said.

The photographer turned at the same moment as Gideon and edged closer.

"Trish," Gideon acknowledged. He sighed inwardly. It needed only this to cap off the evening. But better that he saw her now, when he was minutes away from leaving, rather than spending the whole night trying to avoid her.

She traced the rim of her wine glass with a manicured finger. "I see ginger ale is still your beverage of choice at social events."

"That's right," he answered, taking a small sip as he watched her warily.

"Are you here alone?"

The photographer held his breath as he waited for Gideon's answer.

"Yes."

"Me too. I came with some friends—but I'm not obligated to stay with them."

Was she coming on to him? His defenses on high alert, he took a step back, his eyes scanning the area past her. He spied the photographer and shot a suspicious glance at Trish.

The photographer moved forward and flashed his press credentials. "Mind if I take a couple of pictures?"

Gideon and Trish obligingly posed, although Gideon was careful to angle his body away from hers. The shots taken, the photographer thanked them and then set off in search of other game.

Gideon rotated towards the pool and drained the last of his ginger ale.

Trish sidled around and looked up speculatively at Gideon. "I haven't seen or heard your name linked with anyone else's."

"Oh? I haven't paid attention to celebrity gossip lately."

"I hope you're not still carrying the torch for me, as the saying goes," she said coyly.

He looked down at her and laughed humorlessly. "No, that torch burned out a long time ago."

Trish's simper faded.

Forgive her, Gideon.

He resisted the command. He *wanted* to hold onto that grudge; he *wanted* her to feel a portion of the hurt and embarrassment she had inflicted on him. But, as Trish started to move away, Gideon yielded, his features softening. "I'm sorry, Trish… I didn't mean to hurt you. The truth is, I've moved on. Based on what you said in that television interview last year, I thought you had already moved on, too."

"I *thought* I had." She turned to him then, looking at him resolutely. "I've wanted to apologize for that interview. I know I said some things I shouldn't have. I was too caught up in myself."

"It's all forgiven. In the long run, you did us both a favor. That's the way I choose to look at it, anyway."

"So there's no going back?"

"I'm afraid not," he replied gently.

"Oh," she said, looking down at her wineglass.

Now comfort her.

"Trish."

She raised her eyes to his.

"I'm going to give you the same advice someone gave me last year. Be patient. The right person is out there and you *will* find him," he said earnestly.

She gave a nod and searched his face. "You've changed, Gideon. You seem… more at peace. I guess that advice worked for you."

"It's early days yet but, yeah, I'm happy."

"I'm glad for you."

"Thanks."

"Take your glass, sir?" a waiter asked.

He flashed a grateful smile and set the glass on the proffered tray. As the waiter moved away, Gideon turned back to Trish and touched her shoulder lightly. "It was nice to see you, Trish. Take care."

"You, too," she answered.

He felt strangely lighthearted as he reentered the house and maneuvered his way through the crowd. *I really have forgiven her.* Pausing only to thank his host and hostess, he climbed the steps to the foyer and passed through the front door.

As the valet summoned his town car, he typed a quick text to Kendra.

Duty fulfilled. I'm glad you made me go.

Minutes later, ensconced in the back seat of the town car, he sent a FaceTime request.

Mallory looked up from her laptop when her phone pinged. She smiled when she saw Gideon's name.

"Hi," she greeted when his face appeared.

"Hi. You look like you're hard at work."

"Yeah. What about you?"

"I'm on my way home."

"Already?"

"Yeah—Kendra and I made a deal that I would only have to stay for a little while."

"So how was the party?"

He shrugged, saying, "It was the typical Hollywood bash." He grinned. "Except that the party was at a house that was made to look like Roman ruins. I've never seen so many columns and arches and niches in my life! I wish you had been with me to see it."

Mallory grimaced. "Oh my. Either the homeowners were very specific in what they wanted, or their architect went rogue."

Gideon laughed. "I think it was a little of both."

At that moment, Lettie's name popped up on Mallory's phone. "Hang on a second—Lettie just sent me a text." Toggling to Lettie's multimedia message, Mallory's eyes widened. She typed a quick response and then returned to Face Time. "Oh my gosh, Gideon! Lettie and Ethan are engaged!"

Gideon merely grinned.

"You knew!"

He chuckled. "Yeah, Ethan told me he was going to ask her tonight. He was nervous about it, but I had no doubt what her answer would be. They're perfect for each other. And speaking of perfect couples, there's something I need to tell you about Rachel and Gareth's wedding…"

CHAPTER 13

Saturday, November 2ⁿᵈ

"So *why* do we need to go shopping today?" Lettie asked as she met Mallory on a busy sidewalk. "I thought you were having a cookout with Gideon's family."

"I am, but that's five hours from now. Gideon told me last night that Rachel wants the wedding party and their spouses or dates to be color-coordinated."

"Right: plum or lavender dresses for the women and black suits or tuxes with plum or lavender ties for the men. Apparently the only exceptions will be Rachel and her mom," Lettie said, turning and falling into step with her cousin.

"I don't have a dress in either of those colors, and this is about the only free day I have to shop for one," she replied. *And even now, I really can't afford to take the time*, she thought, thinking about her assignment to design a seamless addition for an actual structure that was at least 30 years old. Some of her classmates had found mid-century modern homes or California bungalows as the basis for their project, but she wanted something different—she just didn't know what.

"You could always sew your own," Lettie said, pulling her back to the moment.

Mallory shook her head. "No, I would feel too rushed to get it done. It's better to just buy one." *And hopefully it won't be too expensive.* She didn't want to dip into the money she'd been setting aside to buy Christmas presents for her family.

"I was going to wear a lavender dress I've had for a few years, but if you're getting a new dress, I just may have to buy one too! Are you looking for something short or long?"

"At this point, I really don't have a preference." She paused at one of the windows fronting a bridal shop. "I thought we'd start here. This is where Rachel said she found the bridesmaid dresses. Who knows? Maybe you'll get some ideas for your own wedding."

But Lettie's attention was fixed on the woman who was dressing the store window. "Wow, I never realized bridal shops decorated for Christmas too!" The cousins watched for a moment and then moved to the store entrance.

"Lettie," Mallory said musingly, drawing out the second syllable of her cousin's name. "Remember how we insisted on having matching Easter and Christmas dresses every year when we were growing up?"

Lettie laughed as she reached for the door. "I sure do! Those were the only times of the year I could pretend that the two of us were twins, instead of you and Max!" She stopped. "Wait. Are you thinking what I *think* you're thinking?"

Mallory tilted her head and spread out her hands. "Well, the bridesmaids are going to be wearing identical dresses, and Gideon and his brothers and Ethan are going to have matching tuxes, so…"

"…there's no reason why you and I can't be dressed alike!" Lettie finished, giving her cousin a high-five.

It was just before five o'clock when Gideon pulled his SUV into the driveway and drew into the leftmost bay of the three-car garage, which was set back about ten feet from the two-car section that housed the Impala and Gareth's vehicle. Gideon pushed the button on the remote, and the garage door lowered. "Ready?" he asked Mallory.

"I guess so."

They opened their respective doors and got out of the car. Sensing her nervousness, he put his arm around her as he guided her to the side door. "Don't worry. It'll be fine," he assured her as he opened the door for her.

She nodded, stepped through the doorway, and stopped. Because of its offset position, she'd assumed this was just a shorter bay whose back wall was flush with the back side of the two-car garage. Instead, she realized the back wall was also offset, forming a reverse L, and she and Gideon were standing on a concrete walkway that ran between the two-car unit on the right and a landscape bed on the left before curving around to the back door of the house. She turned and scanned the roofline of the garage with growing excitement.

"What's wrong?"

"Gideon, what year was your house built?"

"1991, I believe."

"Do you think your dad would mind if I took some pictures and made some measurements of the garage?"

"No, of course not. But... why?"

"I have an assignment to pretend that it's the year 2175 and that I've been hired to add a second story living space to an existing 1-story 20th century structure. The goal is to preserve as much of the original building as possible, and make the addition seem like it's always been there. Seeing the footprint of your garage has given me an idea." She strode back and forth along the walkway as she studied the garage. "This would be perfect!"

"Another job for Super Designer Woman," he grinned. "How can I help?"

"Do you have a tape measure in your garage?"

He chuckled. "Sure. Just a minute."

Eagerly, Mallory pulled out her cell phone and began taking pictures.

"Mallory? Is everything all right? I saw you and Gideon pull into the driveway but when you didn't come in, I started to worry," Garrison said as he approached her from the house.

"Yes, everything's fine," she assured him, grasping his outstretched hand.

"I found two tape measures: a twenty-five foot one and a fifty-foot one," Gideon announced, holding one in each hand.

"The fifty-foot one would be better, probably."

"Mallory has a design assignment and she wants to base it on our garage," Gideon explained to his father as he clipped the unwanted tape measure to his belt.

"*If* that's okay," Mallory interposed, looking up at Garrison. "I promise I won't use your name or address." She held up her phone. "I just have to be able to prove that it's an actual building. The pictures will do that."

"Yes, that would be fine. I'm curious to see what you do. Can I help?"

"Sure. Why don't you and Gideon do the measuring and I'll draw a rough outline for my notes?" She reached into her purse and pulled out a small memo book and a pen.

"Sounds like a plan. Where do you want us to start?"

"Right here would be fine," she said, using her pen to point to the back wall of the 2-car garage.

Gareth and Rachel arrived while Gideon and his dad were measuring the position of a window on the leftmost bay.

"What's going on?" Gareth asked.

"Taking some measurements," Garrison answered, running the tape measure up to the top of the window casing. "Yes, this one's the same."

"Got it," Mallory replied, making a notation before leading the way to the driveway.

"I can *see* you're taking measurements, but *why*?" Gareth asked as he and Rachel followed the others. Gideon quickly explained Mallory's assignment as Mallory aimed her phone.

After she had snapped the last of her pictures, Gideon and Garrison moved forward to take the final set of measurements.

By five-twenty-five, Gabriel and his family had not arrived yet, but everyone else was bustling around, getting things ready for the cookout. While Garrison tended the grill, Gareth and Rachel wiped down the large dining table under the pergola, and Graham and Shannon followed behind them, laying out placemats and silverware.

"Oh, Mallory, you don't have to do that," Garrison protested when he came back inside and found Mallory helping Gideon slice vegetables and place them on a sectioned tray while baby Avery watched from her high chair.

"You told me to make myself at home." she reminded with a twinkle as he walked behind her to the counter next to the refrigerator.

Knife clasped in one hand, Gideon mopped his watering eyes with his forearm. "Well come on, then," he said, offering the knife and partially sliced onion to her. "I'll be glad to let you take over for me."

"Sure," she answered, reaching for the knife.

"Wimp," Gabriel teased as he and Courtney walked in, Courtney holding Jesse and David's hands and Gabriel carrying a guitar case.

Gideon snatched his hands away from Mallory's reach. "Never let it be said that I'm a wimp when it comes to slicing onions," he laughed.

As Gabriel set down his guitar case, Jesse and David broke away from their mom and ran to hug Garrison's legs. "Easy, boys," Garrison said, uncovering the platter of hamburger and hot dog buns. He picked up the platter and smiled down at his grandsons. "Almost time to eat."

"Yay!" they chorused.

Courtney greeted Mallory and introduced her to Gabriel and their youngest son, David.

"So *you're* the one who fixed Jesse's costume—and saved Gideon from the doghouse," Gabriel said, tossing a mischievous look at his brother.

"I'm just glad there wasn't any irreparable damage."

"Well, you sure have made an impression on Jesse. It's been *Mall'ry this* and *Mall'ry that* ever since then."

"I was happy to help," Mallory answered. She staggered slightly as Jesse flung his arms around her, and, laughing, she bent to return the hug. *Oh, how I miss Cassidy and Jeremy.*

Shannon opened the back door and leaned inside. "Okay, everyone, it's time."

Moments later, they had taken their seats around the dining table. At Garrison's prompting, Jesse and David recited the familiar children's prayer:

> God is great, God is good.
> Let us thank Him for our food.
> By His hand we are fed.
> Give us, Lord, our daily bread.

Dinner was a lighthearted affair filled with cheerful banter. Jesse and David ate quickly and then, at their father's suggestion, hopped down from the table and played tag, chasing each other around the back yard as the grownups chatted. From time to time Shannon, a professional photographer whose camera was never far from hand, snapped candid shots. Although Gideon's firm grasp on her hand helped Mallory endure the moments when Shannon's camera pointed in their direction, she still could not bring herself to look directly into the lens.

The sun was starting its downward arc toward the fiery-hued horizon when the grownups at last rose from the table. Gideon considered showing Mallory the studio, but she was already helping Shannon clear the plates and silverware as Courtney and Gabriel gathered up the glasses.

It can wait until another time.

"Hey, you *could* help, you know," Gareth teased. Flashing an answering smile, Gideon joined Gareth and Rachel in bringing the leftover food into the kitchen while Garrison picked up Avery and rounded up the boys. As Gideon entered the kitchen, his eyes immediately went to Mallory, who was in quiet conversation with Shannon. He smiled to himself. *I'm so glad she's comfortable with everyone.*

Minutes later, the dishes placed in the dishwasher and the food put away, Gabriel picked up his guitar case and led the way into the family room. Mallory looked up at Gideon questioningly as they fell in behind the others. "Family singalong," Gideon explained with a grin.

"Which Avery is going to miss," Graham commented, taking his sleeping daughter from Garrison's arms. "I'll join you in a minute," he said, taking the diaper bag from Shannon before turning and carrying Avery into the living room, where a play yard had been set up.

Gabriel tuned his guitar while everyone claimed seats on the furniture or, like Gideon and Mallory, sat on the floor. "Here's one for the kids," he said, smiling when, delighted, they recognized the opening strains to "Itsy-Bitsy Spider." Gideon watched in amusement as Mallory and Courtney helped Jesse and David with the hand motions. Graham slipped into the family room and sat beside

Shannon as Gabriel led in to "Wheels on the Bus" followed by "She'll Be Coming 'Round the Mountain." Garrison then suggested the four brothers sing one of the songs they'd be performing in Branson. Standing and arranging themselves in the formation they had used since their earliest performances, they obliged with "O Holy Night." By the end of the carol, Jesse and David had also drifted off, and they, too, were carried into the living room and settled on the sofa.

"Now here's one for Gideon," Gabriel said later, strumming the beginning of "Little Drummer Boy." Gideon laughed, but urged the others to join him.

"How about one for the girls," Gareth suggested next.

"Okay. 'Silver Bells' maybe?" Gabriel asked. Shannon, Courtney, and Rachel murmured their agreement.

"You too, Mallory," Rachel said, tugging her arm to pull her to her feet.

From her earliest memories Mallory had enjoyed singing. Over the years, she had sung in church choirs, school choruses, and, during her freshman year of college, even musical theater. The crushing events she'd experienced had brought a halt to that. For the first six months following her retreat home, she had stopped singing altogether. Then, as the holiday season had approached, she began tentatively to sing the beloved carols to herself or at home with her immediate family. Midway through the following year, she had finally mustered the courage to sing along with the congregation during Sunday worship service.

But now, while it had been one thing to sing unison with Gideon's entire family, she had qualms about singing with just the women. Hesitantly she joined Shannon, Courtney, and Rachel next to Gabriel and listened as he strummed the lilting introduction. Her heart sank. The key, while suitable for Shannon, Courtney, and Rachel's soprano voices, was pitched too high for Mallory's alto. She would have to sing harmony, and while the part was one she had sung countless times before, it meant that her voice would stand out from the other women's.

The introduction was over; it was time to sing.

Self-consciously at first, then with growing confidence and enjoyment, she voiced the familiar lyrics. The second verse began, and she noticed Gabriel raising his eyebrows at Graham.

Am I singing too loudly? Her voice faltered, and she cut her eyes to Gideon, who winked at her reassuringly and motioned upward with one hand. This was just an impromptu sing-along, she reminded herself—no one, least of all she, was expected to sing his or her best. The important thing was the camaraderie, the joy of being together. And so she sang stronger, once more becoming absorbed in the music and lyrics.

When the song ended, Gideon led the applause. "Well done," he said, squeezing her hand as she sat back down beside him.

She shook her head deprecatingly and held a finger to her lips as Gabriel gently strummed the lead-in to "Silent Night."

"It was a lot of fun being with your family," Mallory said as she and Gideon pulled out of the driveway and headed towards her apartment. "Thank you so much for inviting me."

He reached over and took her hand. "I'm glad you came."

"So are the family singalongs a tradition in your family?"

"Yes, we've had them for as long as I can remember. They started out as a way to practice our songs for Sunday school and children's choir and Vacation Bible School at church. As we got a little older, Mom and Dad began teaching us simple harmonies. Later on, they were a way for us to practice playing our instruments and singing at the same time." He gave a wry laugh. "And the next thing my brothers and I knew, we were officially a boy band."

"'Boy Band'—I hate that term."

He glanced over at her in surprise. "I do too."

"So what church do you go to? Would it be all right if I went with you some time?"

He waited until he had merged the car into traffic before finally saying, "Actually, we don't go to church anymore. Once we started performing professionally, things just got really strange. We'd be sitting in the congregation and when it was time for a hymn, most people wouldn't sing—they would just watch and listen to us. And the choir seemed self-conscious about singing in front of us, too. As we started touring, weeks might go by before we would be back home and able to attend services, which seemed to ruffle some feathers. The pastor finally told my parents that it would probably be better if we found another church. Instead, we stopped going altogether."

"That is so sad," Mallory said, shaking her head. "I can't believe your pastor actually told you to go somewhere else."

"Well, to be fair, he was young and hadn't been at our church very long—in fact, our church was his first appointment as a pastor. He was also from the Midwest, so I guess he didn't realize how anyone with any degree of popularity would affect his flock."

Mallory nodded pensively. "Maybe so. It's a shame, though."

"Yeah," he agreed with a sigh. Silence stretched between them as Gideon debated whether to say more. Knowing how much her faith meant to her, he was hesitant to confess his weakness, afraid she would think less of him. He released her hand as he eased off the freeway and prepared to turn at the light. Straightening the wheel, he said at last, "I have to admit I drifted away from God a few years ago. I was hurt and sad and angry, and I blamed God for it." He braked for a light and looked over at her. "I guess that's hard for you to understand."

She grabbed his arm. "Are you kidding? That's *exactly* how I felt. Even though I came off relatively unscathed compared to other women who have been attacked, I was traumatized. I kept asking God where He had been, why He had abandoned me. It took a long time to understand that He had been with me all along." She peered at him, trying to read his expression in the dim light cast by the car's instrument panel. "You understand that now, too… don't you?"

He took his left hand from the steering wheel and placed it atop Mallory's hand.

God, what a gift you've brought to me in this woman.

"Yes," he said softly. "I understand now."

Lettie and Ethan looked up when Mallory and Gideon entered the apartment.

Ethan pressed Pause on the remote. "You're just in time. We're getting ready to watch 'Dial M for Murder'."

"Yes, come join us!"

Mallory looked up at Gideon. "Can you stay?"

"Yes, I'd love to," he said. "I haven't seen that in a long time."

"I haven't either. It's one of my favorite Alfred Hitchcock movies. But I want to get something to drink first. Want one?"

"Yes, please," he said, following her.

"We'll give you two minutes," Ethan called after them.

"Oh, and Mallory, you've got some mail. Looks like birthday cards from your family," Lettie added.

"Your birthday?" Gideon asked once they were in the kitchen.

"On Tuesday."

"Why didn't you tell me?"

"We just started seeing each other, Gideon. I didn't want you to feel obligated to get me anything."

"I appreciate that, but the whole point of dating is learning more about each other. Knowing your birthday is just one more thing to celebrate together."

"You're right—I'm sorry." She handed him a soda can. "So when's *your* birthday?"

"Oh, now *that* is a state secret. If I told you, you'd have to go into the witness protection program," he teased, pulling the tab on the can.

"Ten seconds," Ethan warned.

"Coming," Gideon answered. He and Mallory walked into the living room and Ethan and Lettie made room for them on the sofa. Once they were seated, Gideon leaned towards her and placed his right hand against his chest. "June 17th," he whispered. He held up his can. "To birthdays."

"To birthdays," she answered, touching her can to his before taking a sip.

CHAPTER 14

Monday, November 4th

Mallory pressed the phone against her ear with one hand and rubbed her forehead with the other. "Hi, Max, it's me—again. It's three o'clock here, so that means it's six o'clock back home. You must be really, *really* celebrating. I miss you. Call me." Ending the call, she tossed the phone onto the sofa cushion and leaned her head back, closing her eyes.

What a lousy birthday.

The apartment door opened and Lettie entered quietly. "You're up! I hope this means your migraine is almost gone?"

"Yes—finally."

"Still fuzzy-headed, huh?"

"A little." She stood up. "I'm going to take a shower. Maybe the steam will knock the last of it out."

"Well, don't take too long… Gideon will be here in about an hour." Seeing the expression on her cousin's face, she added, "You really *are* fuzzy-headed if you forgot that. Go get your shower. I'll have some hot peppermint tea ready when you're done."

"Thanks, Lettie."

─────────────

Gideon and Ethan were seated with Lettie at the dining table when Mallory walked into the kitchen. The sliding door to the balcony was open, the long curtains billowing playfully in the breeze.

"Gideon, Ethan—hi!"

"I'm early, I know," Gideon said apologetically.

"No, that's fine—I'm glad you're here."

He watched as she gratefully accepted the mug of tea from Lettie before settling on the vacant dining room chair across from him.

"Lettie was telling us about your migraine. My mom used to get them once or twice a month, so I know how miserable they can be. Are you feeling better?"

"Yes, much better." She took a sip of tea and cradled the warm mug in her hands.

"I've never had peppermint tea before."

"I haven't either. It's pretty good," Ethan remarked, taking a sip.

"My mom is a firm believer in herbal teas. She always gave us peppermint tea when we had colds or the flu… or in my case, after a migraine."

"I'll have to remember that," Gideon commented. "It sure clears the sinuses."

Lettie's phone dinged. Without looking at it, she picked it up from the table and stuffed it in her back pocket as she stood up. "You know what? I forgot to check the mail when I got home. Why don't you come with me, Ethan?"

He drank the last of his tea and set down his mug. "Okay."

Mallory exchanged a smile with Gideon over the brim of her mug before taking another small swallow of the fragrant brew. Gideon pushed his mug to one side and reached behind him. "I was going to give this to you at dinner, but I decided not to wait," he said, placing a small gift bag on the table and sliding it towards her. "Happy birthday."

"Oh, Gideon! I told you I didn't want you to feel obligated to get me something!"

"I didn't feel obligated—it's something I wanted to do."

Setting down her mug, she reached into the bag and pulled out a wad of tissue paper. "It's kind of heavy." Placing it gently on the table, she pulled back the tissue. "Oh, a paperweight!" she exclaimed, holding up a glass turtle, its head and legs just visible from the shell.

"It reminded me of what you said the day of our picnic."

"About being like a turtle—yes, exactly! I can't believe you remembered that. This is so sweet of you," she said, still clutching the paperweight as she jumped up from her chair. He stood as she rounded the table to him.

"So tell me: is it going in or coming out of its shell?"

Karen Lail

"Oh, definitely out," she answered, stepping into his embrace. "Thank you!"

"You're welcome." He looked at her upturned face. *Is it still too soon?* Watching her for signs of hesitation, he gradually bent his head and touched her lips with his, breathing in the scent of peppermint.

"Special delivery!" Lettie sang out.

Gideon and Mallory pulled apart.

Who in the world… Gideon wondered. Realization dawned as Mallory let out a soft squeal and flew across the room to greet the young man and middle-aged couple who had entered with Lettie and Ethan. He followed her but stood apart, not wanting to intrude on the reunion.

"I can't believe you're here!" she exclaimed, hugging each one in turn.

"We wanted to surprise you," Roger said.

"Well, you succeeded," she laughed. She walked to Gideon, looped her arm through his, and brought him forward. "Gideon, these are my parents, Roger and Meredythe, and my brother, Max. Mom, Dad, Max… this is Gideon Locke."

"Call me Roger," her father said, warmly shaking his hand.

"And I'm Meredythe. It's so nice to meet you, Gideon."

"It's nice to meet you, too." He turned to Mallory's brother and held out his hand. "Hi, Max. I've heard a lot about you."

Max cast a glance of swift appraisal at him as he grasped Gideon's hand. "Ditto," he replied, his smile not quite reaching his eyes.

So Max is reserving judgment.

"I guess Lettie has already introduced you to her fiancé, Ethan?" Mallory asked.

"Yes, we met downstairs," Meredythe replied with a smile at Ethan.

"Well, come in and sit down!" Lettie urged. She and Ethan moved ahead and carried two of the dining chairs into the living room.

Mallory paused and turned to her brother as their parents moved past them. "I've been trying to reach you all day. Why didn't you answer me?"

Max looked down at Mallory. "Uh, hello—what part of 'surprise' do you not understand?"

She hit her brother's arm. "Stop."

He grinned and enfolded her in another hug. "Happy birthday, sis."

"Happy birthday."

They separated, and Mallory, her cheeks flushed with excitement, cast a smile at Gideon as he slipped his arm around her.

"So what brings you to Los Angeles?" she asked as they settled in the living room—Roger, Meredythe, and Max on the sofa; the others on the chairs.

"Your dad had a convention in San Francisco. Max and I decided to tag along and do some sightseeing, so Aidan is taking care of the practice while we're all away. The three of us took a commuter flight down here shortly after lunchtime," Meredythe explained.

Mallory shot a glance at her brother. "So you're playing hooky?"

"Yes, but with the blessing of my professors," Max assured her.

Lettie took up the story. "Max told me a few days ago that they were coming to surprise you, and said he would text me as soon as the taxi dropped them off here."

"Oh, so *that's* why you suddenly had to check the mail?"

"Yep."

Gideon's phone rang. He pulled it out and checked the caller ID. "I need to take this. Excuse me," he said, getting up and striding out to the balcony as he put the phone to his ear. "Hi, Kendra."

Without preamble, Kendra asked, "Gideon, is there something going on with you and Trish Galloway that I should know about?"

"No! Why do you ask?"

"I've been inundated with requests for a comment about whether the two of you have reconciled."

"What? Kendra, I promise you, nothing is going on. We posed for a couple of pictures at Dirk and Kate's party, but there was nothing to it—it was just the usual publicity stuff."

"So no intimate moments? No hugs, no air kisses?"

"Absolutely not! We talked a little, and she apologized for the things she'd done, and I told her I forgive her. That's all that happened."

"Okay, if that's all it was, I'll prepare a statement. Is it fair to say that although you and Trish parted on bad terms last year, the two of you have been able to move past that and can now meet each other amicably?"

"Yes, I'd say that sums it up."

"You know, Gideon, the way to put all these rumors about you and Trish to rest once and for all would be to admit you're dating someone else."

"*No!*" he exclaimed, panicked. He pulled himself together and continued, more restrained, "No, I'd like to wait until after the wedding, if possible."

"Okay. I'll put this together and send it to you in a couple of minutes."

"Thanks, Kendra." He tucked his phone in his back pocket and, sighing, leaned on the railing.

A moment later, he realized he was no longer alone.

"Mind if I join you?" Max asked.

"Not at all."

He came to the railing and, like Gideon, leaned his forearms on it and looked out over the parking lot.

Gideon waited one beat, two beats, three… At last, he swiveled his head to the right. "Get it off your chest, Max."

Max heard the note of weariness in Gideon's voice and felt a moment's regret that he was about to add to Gideon's burden. He considered quashing his reservations and leaving Gideon in peace. But this might be the only time he would have alone with Gideon; the only way he could protect Mallory. He met Gideon's gaze. "I'm just trying to figure you out. I read all this stuff about you and think you're just the typical shallow self-gratifying celebrity, but then I see you with my sister and think maybe you're not such a bad guy after all."

Gideon didn't answer, just looked at Max steadily.

Emboldened by that unwavering gaze, Max pulled out his phone and brought up a screen shot he had saved. "If you're supposedly dating my sister, how do you explain this?" he demanded, thrusting the phone towards Gideon.

It was a picture of Gideon and Trish from Dirk and Kate's party, the moment when Gideon had touched her shoulder as he said goodbye to her. But the angle of the camera, the soft glow on their faces from the light of the fire pit, suggested a more intimate interaction.

This, then, was the reason Kendra was being inundated with calls.

Gideon met Max's questioning look squarely.

"Oh, there you are," Meredythe said brightly as Gideon and Max returned from the balcony.

Mallory smiled up at Gideon as he perched on the arm of her chair. "Mom and Dad were just telling me that they can only stay for one night."

"Oh? That doesn't give you much time to spend together," he replied, looking from Mallory to her parents.

"Well, technically we don't have to be back until Thursday," Roger stated, "but I have a couple of cataract surgeries scheduled for Friday morning, and I wanted to have a day to get reacclimated to East Coast time. So we'll fly out very early tomorrow morning—which means we'll have to get to the airport around four or four-thirty a.m."

"But we were hoping we could take you out to dinner for your birthday before we head back to our hotel," Meredythe said.

"Actually, Mom—"

Gideon took Mallory's hand in his and squeezed it gently. "It's okay. We can go out another night. You need to be with your family."

"But—"

"It's okay," he repeated, drawing out his phone. "There's still time to cancel our reservation."

Roger's gaze toggled between Gideon and Mallory. "Is there any chance we could change your reservation from a party of two to a party of seven—for all of us?" he asked, his glance encompassing Lettie and Ethan.

"Oh, Roger, look how dressed up Mallory and Gideon are. You and Max and I would have to go all the way back to the hotel to change for dinner, and I'm selfish enough to want to spend that time with our daughter instead."

"You're right, hon." He looked at Gideon apologetically. "I hate to ruin your dinner plans, but how about if we just have something delivered here? We'd really like to spend time with all of you," he said, his gaze again including Ethan and Lettie.

"Thanks for the invitation Roger, but Lettie and I are having dinner with my parents tonight," Ethan replied as he rose from his chair.

"Yes, we're starting to make wedding plans," Lettie explained.

"It was very nice to meet you," Ethan continued, stretching out his hand to grasp first Roger's, then Meredythe's, and finally Max's hand.

"You'll probably be gone by the time I get home, so I'll go ahead and say goodbye to you now, too," Lettie said, moving forward to hug her aunt and uncle.

"What about you, Gideon? Will you join us?" Meredythe asked as the door closed behind Ethan and Lettie.

Mallory looked at him hopefully.

His gaze rested briefly on Max before meeting Meredythe's eyes. "If you're sure I won't be intruding on your reunion, I'd love to. Thank you."

"And for the food you have provided and for everyone who is gathered here to partake of it, we are truly thankful. In Jesus' name, amen," Roger said.

"Amen," Gideon chorused with the others. He'd been clasping Mallory's left hand and Meredythe's right during the prayer. Both women gently squeezed his hand, emphasizing each syllable of their "Amens." Undoubtedly this was a Glencoe family custom. *Nice*, he thought as he gave two answering squeezes. Shooting a quick smile at Meredythe before releasing her, he retained his hold on Mallory's hand a fraction of a beat longer, his eyes fixed on hers. The moment passed; realizing her family was watching them, Mallory dipped her head shyly and reached for her fork.

Gideon picked up his own fork. "Mallory told me you own and

operate an eye clinic," he remarked as he speared a broccoli floret.

"Yes, that was our dream from the time Meredythe and I started dating in college. We were very blessed to be able to make it come true," Roger said, covering Meredythe's hand with his and sharing a smile with her. "We've been doubly blessed to have our oldest son, Aidan, come into the practice with us."

"What about you, Max? Will you be joining the practice, too?" Gideon asked.

Max gave a bark of rueful laughter. "Well, that was the original plan. When I finished my junior year of undergraduate school, though, I realized I just didn't have any interest in going to medical school."

"So what did you do? Did you start over with something else?"

"Well, I was minoring in computer science and really enjoyed it. So I ended up changing my major to that, even though it meant having to go to school through the summer."

"Max is the one who brought our medical records system into the 21st century," Roger interjected.

"Oh, nice. So are you working somewhere now?"

"Actually, after I graduated, I decided I wanted to specialize in cybersecurity, so I applied and was accepted into a program at a small college in Albany." Max's eyes touched on Mallory's for a moment. "I ended up delaying my admission by a year, but it just means that Mallory and I should be getting our degrees at around the same time now."

"Cybersecurity. Wow, that sounds intriguing."

"Yeah, it's pretty cool stuff."

"What does your father do, Gideon?" Roger asked.

"He's a semi-retired investment advisor. He used to be with one of the larger brokerage firms, but he went independent once we started touring. He still has a handful of clients he works with, but mostly he helps us with our investments."

"So he's not your agent, or manager, or whatever it's called?"

"Oh, no—he had no interest in doing that. He and my mom would always go along on our tours as our chaperones, and they've always been involved in protecting our brand, but as far as scheduling engagements, coordinating logistics, or handling promotions, we have other folks who help with that. Dad just made sure whatever funds we earned were held in trust until we came of age. Once Gareth turned twenty-one, Dad had us form a limited-liability company for our business and he oversees that for us. He also advises us on our personal portfolios to make sure the funds grow and last as long as possible, without too much risk."

"So you still go on tours?" Max asked.

"Yes, usually three or four weeks in the summer. We'll start somewhere on the east coast and work our way back west, trying to hit different cities or states with each tour. We also do limited engagements in Branson or Vegas or Tahoe once or twice a year."

"You know, Gideon," Meredythe remarked, "Lettie's mother and I took the girls to see your Christmas concert at Madison Square Garden about ten years ago."

"Oh really? Mallory didn't tell me that. I hope you liked it."

"We sure did, even though there was a lot of screaming."

He chuckled. "Well, I can assure you, our performances aren't that noisy now. Our audience has grown up, just like we have. I have to say, though, I miss certain aspects of our early years as a group."

"Oh? Like what?" Roger asked.

"There was a kind of innocence back then. While the teen magazines did have their own agenda, they weren't looking for scandals like the mainstream media; there wasn't the prevalence of fake news like today. We could go out on stage, perform our hearts out, sign some autographs and pose for some pictures, and then it was on to the next stop of the tour. But once Gabriel got married, that all changed. The mainstream media realized we were growing up, and they started following us at about the same time the teen magazines dropped us for some fresh faces. It changed everything. We've learned the hard way that tabloids are not very kind." He met Max's gaze. "It didn't help that I made some choices in my past dating life that I'm not proud of."

"We've *all* made choices we're not proud of," Max acknowledged.

"With all that attention, how can you have any kind of private life?" Meredythe asked, her gaze shifting from Gideon to Mallory.

Gideon and Mallory shared a look before Gideon turned his head back to Meredythe. "It's a challenge. But with my brother's wedding coming up on the sixteenth, he and his fiancée have been the focus of the media's attention, so I've had a bit of a reprieve the past couple of months. Once they're married, though…" He shrugged. "For the most part, I try to ignore the reporters and the paparazzi, but every now and then a story will appear that makes you wonder how they dream this stuff up."

"I can't imagine living in the public eye so much," Meredythe commented.

"It must be very hard to have any type of balance in your life," Roger agreed. "If you ever want to get away for a while, feel free to come to our little town."

"I appreciate that, Roger. We've already got commitments lined up through July, though, so it wouldn't be any time soon."

"By July, Mallory should have graduated and moved back home to open her own design firm," Max remarked. He shot a look at Gideon. "You *did* know that's her plan, right?"

"Of course he knows, Max. I told him the day we met," Mallory said, looking at Gideon for corroboration.

"Oh, yes. Yes, you did."

As he practiced his drum solo, Gideon thought about his conversation with Mallory's family.

Her parents had been immediately accepting of him. He'd had the satisfaction of seeing Max's reserve melt away. But his mind kept replaying Mallory's words, matching them to the cadence: "Of course he knows… I told him the day we met."

He struck a rim shot and, anguished, tossed the sticks aside and clutched his head.

How could I have forgotten that?

And then another thought popped into his head: *Is there any point in continuing to see her?*

Pictures of Mallory cycled through his head like a slide show:

Mallory looking up at him when he stopped her from leaving the game; Mallory bursting into laughter at his lame foreign accent; Mallory smiling as they made their escape from the restaurant; Mallory throwing the football with Rachel at their picnic; Mallory's delight at the paperweight he'd given her; the all-too-brief kiss before her parents had arrived; their second kiss when he had said goodnight.

Yes, it was worth it to go on, to cherish this time with her.

And, please, God, change her mind about leaving LA.

CHAPTER 15

Friday, November 15th

Lettie poked her head into Mallory's bedroom. "I'm heading to class. See you this evening."

Mallory raised her eyes from her laptop. "Have a good day."

"You too. Don't work too hard."

"Easier said than done."

"I know what you mean. Bye!"

Mallory leaned forward in her desk chair and studied the 3-D full perspective rendering on her laptop screen. Moving the mouse, she slowly rotated the image of the Locke family garage. The railing of a covered balcony aligned with the front of the two-car section, stretching back six-and-a-half feet to the exterior wall of the new second story.

She switched to the image of the garage level. A 2-story addition to the rear exterior squared off the back of the garage and formed the private, fully enclosed entrance to the apartment above. An L-shaped staircase started to the left of the side door leading from the single-car bay and rose along the new exterior wall, whose evenly spaced clerestory windows allowed light in without sacrificing privacy. The staircase led to a loft, which opened to a deck on the left. Under the loft area was an exterior door sandwiched between a storage area on the left and a mechanical closet on the right. At the top of the staircase was a small niche with a built-in countertop, which could be used as a console or a shelf for folding clothes. To the right of the niche was a laundry closet with space for a stacked washer and dryer, shelving for laundry and cleaning supplies, and a wall-mounted fold-out drying rack. Beyond the laundry closet, a bump out in the loft gallery led to the door of the actual apartment.

She toggled to the interior view of the apartment. The door from the gallery opened into a generous kitchen with full-size appliances. The sink was centered on one side of the island; on the other side the countertop extended ten inches, allowing three adults to sit comfortably. There was an airy bedroom, spacious bathroom, a closet that could be configured for coats or linens, a living room, and a 100 square foot nook that could serve as a dining room, office, or, if walled in, even a guest space. From the nook was a door that opened to the covered balcony.

Satisfied with the design, she sent an email to her professor that summarized her project and attached the photos she'd taken of the garage as well as the software file for the plan. Remembering her promise to Gideon's father, she took screen captures of each rendering from various angles and attached them to a second email.

> Hi, Gideon. I promised your dad I would let
> him see the design for the garage renovation.
> Here are some screen shots to show him. I hope
> he likes them! If he prefers, I can bring my
> laptop and give him a virtual walkthrough of the
> addition. Thank him again for letting me use
> the garage for this project. See you tomorrow.

After sending the email, she closed her laptop. Her gaze settled on the glass paperweight and, smiling, she picked it up, stroking it thoughtfully as she leaned back in her chair. Fridays were typically devoted to her assignments for her various classes. Today, however, she would be working at the library beginning at one o'clock, having traded days with a coworker so that she could go to Rachel and Gareth's wedding tomorrow. As a result, she'd had to refuse Gideon's invitation to the rehearsal dinner tonight, but he had understood. He and Gareth were going to be busy most of the day as well, so she and Gideon had agreed they would just see each other at the church tomorrow.

She glanced at the small decorative clock on her desk as she replaced the paperweight. She had just over four hours before she needed to leave for campus. The morning stretched out before her, and Mallory decided to get a head start on the weekend cleaning.

One by one, Mallory pulled the damp sheets and pillow cases out of the washer section of the combination laundry unit, shook them, and placed them in the dryer section above. She started the dryer. As she placed the next load in the washer she reflected on the past few weeks. From the day of the picnic, she had noticed a quickening in the pace of her life, but in the ten days since her family's visit, life had seemed to shift into high gear. She and Gideon had seen each other almost daily: playing ping-pong or sharing a snack in the student center on campus, having a Game Night with Lettie and Ethan, just sitting here in the apartment and talking, or, until lately, meeting for early morning runs. Gideon even took her to observe a recording session he and his brothers had, and twice more she had joined in family sing-alongs in Gideon's home. All in all, they spent as much time together as their respective schedules would allow, sharing more and more aspects of their lives.

Mallory lifted a pair of her running capris and grimaced, recalling their last morning run, when she'd learned first-hand just how determined fans and photographers could be. She and Gideon were about midway through the course they'd set and had paused to take a breather. A female jogger had come abreast of them, glancing at them as she passed, and then had suddenly circled back to them. "Aren't you Gideon Locke?" the girl had asked, and then declared excitedly, "It *is* you!" Mallory had retreated to the background, content to observe all the different expressions on Gideon's face as he spoke to the girl. The girl asked to take a picture with him; he consented and, while she was busy activating the camera on her phone, he'd glanced at Mallory as if to reassure himself that she was all right. Mallory watched as Gideon posed with the girl; the girl snapped the picture, checked the image, and suddenly swung the phone towards Mallory. Startled, Mallory had spun on her heel and walked quickly back the way she and Gideon had come. "No more photos," she heard Gideon say firmly, and a moment later he was beside Mallory, his hand grasping her elbow reassuringly as they hurried back to the privacy of his car.

Surprisingly, Gideon had never been accosted by anyone when they were on campus. Perhaps it was because he always asked to let him carry one or two of her books so he could blend in with the other students. Maybe it was simply that a school of architecture was one of the last places Gideon was expected to be seen. Whatever the reason, the campus had become the only public place where they could meet freely.

She started the washer and then carried a can of Pledge and a dusting cloth into the living room. Checking the wall clock, she noted the time as she lightly sprayed the cloth: 8:45 a.m.

She had just finished vacuuming and was starting to fill a pail with hot water and Mr. Clean when a knock sounded on the door. She glanced at the kitchen clock: 10:13. She turned off the water, walked to the door, and peered through the peephole. Astonished, she opened the door for Gideon. She was even more shocked by the expression his face—so shocked that at first she didn't realize Gareth was there, too.

"Come on in," she said belatedly. Wordlessly, Gideon stepped inside, but Gareth stayed where he was.

"Gideon wanted me to drop him off here while I run an errand," he explained, glancing at his brother and then giving Mallory a significant look.

"That's fine," she answered, at a loss to understand what Gareth was hinting. But she knew that he and Gideon shared a special bond, and it was obvious that Gareth was concerned about Gideon's mood. "Take whatever time you need—I don't need to head to campus for a couple of hours," Mallory told him.

Gareth clapped Gideon on the shoulder. "I'll be back as soon as I can," he promised, and Gideon nodded. Gareth gave Mallory another pointed look and then turned away.

She closed the door and turned to face Gideon. He tried to speak, then shook his head and took her in his arms. They just stood there holding one another for a long time. *Please, God,* Mallory beseeched silently, *help me to help him.*

At last he drew back and took her hands in his. "Sorry about that," he said, with a travesty of a smile.

"You have nothing to apologize for—*nothing*," she replied, squeezing his hands.

"I was so afraid you wouldn't be here. I—" He broke off and took a deep breath. "Whew!" he said with a tremulous laugh. He paused again to compose himself. "I just needed to see you," he whispered.

Her eyes welling up in response, she slipped her arms around him, holding him close, comforting him as best she could. "I'm glad you came to me," she said softly.

He sighed, and she felt some of the tension go out of him. Reaching up, he cupped the back of her head and felt the ponytail. He twined the silky length around his fingers. "I haven't seen you with a ponytail since the night of our first date." He drew back and smiled down at her. "So what's the occasion?"

"Cleaning house. I was just about to wash the kitchen floor. Want to help?"

"Sure!"

"I was kidding!"

"Well, I wasn't."

"Okay," she said, taking him by the hand and leading him to the kitchen. "But I have to warn you, I don't use a mop. I do it the good old-fashioned way, down on my hands and knees."

"Hey, if you can handle it, so can I."

She opened the cabinet beneath the sink and pulled out two clean rags from the stack she and Lettie kept there. "Choose your weapon."

Gideon grinned and took one of the cloths, then lifted the pail out of the sink, set it on the floor, and knelt down next to it. "Ready when you are."

She knelt down on the other side of the pail. "Okay, hot shot, let's see what you can do."

Gideon was very quiet, giving no clue to his thoughts as they worked side-by-side. Now that she was past her initial astonishment, she wondered what had caused such repressed anguish. Perhaps there had been another disagreement between the brothers—she knew the pressure of getting in as many rehearsal hours as possible before Rachel and Gareth's wedding had been getting to all of them. She stole a glance at him, noting the expression of sorrow. No, something else was troubling him. And so as she washed her side of the floor, she watched for a sign that he was ready to talk.

When Gideon paused, resting back on his on his heels, Mallory stopped as well and waited.

"Gareth and I visited Mom's grave a while ago. We're coming up on four years since her death and since Gareth and Rachel will still be in Hawaii then, he wanted to go to the cemetery today." His mouth twisted. "I don't know why, but being there just brought back all the pain and sadness and anger."

Mallory stretched out a hand to him. "Oh, Gideon. I'm so sorry."

"Do you know the story of how she died?"

She shook her head. "I didn't want to pry."

His thumb stroked the back of her hand as he gathered his thoughts. "Four years ago, the Wednesday after Thanksgiving, we were scheduled to fly to Great Britain for a five-day, three-city tour, starting in Edinburgh and ending in London. All of us were going except for Courtney and the boys—David was just a few weeks old, and Courtney and Gabriel felt he was too young to travel. Mom always enjoyed visiting London, so while Gabriel would be flying back to the States after our final performance, the rest of us were going to stay a few extra days to do some sightseeing before coming home." He shifted his weight smoothly, sitting on the floor, his right forearm resting on his elevated right knee. "Because we were departing from New York City early Wednesday morning, we had flown out from Los Angeles on Tuesday. At two o'clock Wednesday morning, Mom woke up not feeling well—a stomach virus, she thought—and after an hour or so we knew there was no way she could travel. Dad wanted to stay with her, but she convinced him to go ahead as planned, saying she would join us in London in time for our last show. So Dad arranged to extend Mom's stay at the hotel and then we left. Between them, Dad and Courtney called Mom every day to check on her. After the third day, we knew it was more than just a stomach virus—it was the flu. Courtney offered to go to New York to stay with Mom, but Mom was afraid that Courtney or the boys would get it, so she refused, saying she thought the worst was behind her. She was very weak, though, and she decided it would be

Karen Lail

best to just fly home instead of trying to go on to London." A muscle in his jaw twitched. "We had flown in to London from Cardiff, when Dad got word that Mom had collapsed as she got off the plane in Los Angeles. The paramedics were called, and they determined that Mom was severely dehydrated. They started an IV, pumping fluids as fast as they could, and got her in the ambulance, but she died on the way to the hospital—something about her body not having enough blood…" He broke off and shook his head.

"Oh, how awful that she died alone!"

His gaze snapped to hers. Somehow, Mallory had hit on it: the one aspect of his mom's death that continued to haunt all of them, especially Dad. He blinked back tears as he drew a ragged breath. "We decided to go on with the show, knowing Mom would have wanted us to keep that commitment, but I knew I'd have a hard time singing 'Christmas in the Key of G' that night. I'd written that song for her, you know."

"I had no idea—I always thought it was a play on all of your names."

"Yeah, that was the slant the record company took when we chose that for the title of the album. But no: It was all about my mom, Grace, and how she taught us to live, not just at Christmastime but every day."

"So what did you do? I mean, that's your signature song for the holidays. Did you just omit it from the program?"

Long-repressed images from that performance surfaced: starting the song, getting partway through the first verse, his voice cracking. Gabriel quickly stepping out from behind the keyboard, snatching up a mic, striding back and forth across the stage and urging the audience to sing the rest of the verse and the chorus, giving time for Gideon to regain control.

But looking at Mallory, all Gideon said was, "We had the audience sing it with us."

So the audience would cover their voices, she thought.

"I don't remember anything about the rest of the show—we were all on autopilot, I think. While we were performing, Dad was frantically trying to get us all booked on a flight back home. I've never seen him so broken. He still hasn't forgiven himself for not staying behind with her." He paused for a beat and then continued, "Before all of this happened, Gareth and I had been tossing around the idea of moving into our own place together. But once Mom died, we didn't discuss it again—we knew we needed to stay with Dad."

"Of course you did. You all needed each other. Losing her must have been a huge blow."

Again he nodded. "All of us have struggled with it. In fact, this engagement in Branson that we've been rehearsing for will be the first time we've done our holiday show since Mom died. Up until last year, we would all go to St. Thomas from the middle of November through New Year's—we just couldn't stand to be home."

"What was different about last year?"

"Graham and Shannon's baby. Shannon's doctor wouldn't let her travel since she was due in early January. So we stayed home and actually put up the Christmas tree. I'm hoping that this year Dad will feel like doing more decorating. Gareth and I are going to try to get him to, anyway."

"I hope so, too." She paused. "You said when you got here that all the pain and sadness and anger had come back. Does that mean…" She broke off as he leaned in and gave her a quick kiss.

"I miss my mom every day, but there are just some times when the grief seems so fresh and raw, like today. It may be that this will be the cycle of things for the rest of my life—I don't know." He squeezed her hand. "But I do know I'm holding to God's promise that I will see her again someday."

"Good." She squeezed his hand in return. "Thanks for telling me about your mom, Gideon."

"Thanks for listening." He released her hand, plunged his cloth back in the pail, and then playfully flicked water at her. "Let's knock this out, shall we?"

And so they resumed their task, laughing and teasing each other as they slowly backed their way across the floor.

Gideon was carrying the pail of dirty water to the hall bathroom when a tap sounded at the door. "That's probably Gareth," he called over his shoulder.

Karen Lail

"How is he?" Gareth asked as soon as Mallory opened the door.

Hearing Gideon coming down the hall, she murmured, "He *seems* better. But see what you think."

Gareth looked at the pail in Gideon's hand and the damp patch on one knee. "What on earth have *you* been doing?"

"Helping Mallory wash the kitchen floor." He looked at her. "Do you want me to set this outside to dry?"

"I can do that. I know you have to go."

"It'll only take a second," he answered. As Gideon opened the sliding door to the balcony, Gareth looked at Mallory questioningly.

"'Clean house, clean mind'," she quoted, and Gareth nodded.

Gideon joined them at the door and slipped an arm around Mallory as Gareth stepped back a couple of paces to give them a measure of privacy. "Thank you. I feel almost like a normal person."

"You *are* a normal person—it's this business you're in that's crazy."

"It definitely has its moments." He bent to kiss her. "Thank you again. I'll see you tomorrow."

"Ready?" Gareth asked.

"Only if you let *me* drive. I don't know where your mind is today, but you terrify me."

Gareth laughed and handed over the car keys. "It's all yours."

Gideon opened the door and then looked back at her with a grateful smile. "Bye."

"Bye," she answered softly.

Gareth waited while Gideon stepped out in the hall, then took Mallory's hand and squeezed it. "Thank you for being so good for him."

Eyes awash with unshed tears, she could only squeeze his hand in return as she nodded.

He's been good for me, too, she reflected as she closed the door. He had managed to forge through the barriers of her shyness and past hurts, plumbing the depths of her spirit and making it clear he liked what he found.

"I think I'm falling in love with you, Gideon Locke," she murmured, her eyes alight with wonder.

But did he feel the same way? He obviously enjoyed hugging and kissing her. And *such* kisses, born of many different emotions. Sometimes tender. Sometimes teasing. Sometimes triumphant (as when they beat Lettie and Ethan at Rook) or, as she learned today, sometimes tinged with sorrow. And, sometimes, filled with such sweetly exhilarating passion that held the promise of so much more…

Yet—whether due to his upbringing, awareness of the trauma she'd experienced, or the pain and regrets of his own failed relationships—he was careful never to push the boundaries of physical contact. For now, he seemed content to focus on deepening their friendship, seeing this as a time of healing for both of them.

Her face grew solemn.

With just six months remaining before she would graduate and move back to New York, maybe that was all either of them could—or should—hope for.

―――――――――――――――――

The photographer rapidly snapped pictures of Gareth and Gideon as they emerged from the apartment building and got into the SUV. A satisfied smile on his face, he scrolled through the pictures he'd taken that morning. His suspicion that Gareth would visit his mother's grave had paid off in spades. The graveside pictures were good sentimental shots and should bring a nice paycheck.

He'd been fortunate: the brothers were upset just enough not to notice him following them as they left the cemetery and made the trip here. He studied the photos of the brothers walking into the apartment building, Gideon's head bowed, Gareth eyeing him in concern; Gareth exiting and returning alone; Gideon momentarily appearing on a balcony; and finally, the brothers leaving together. Obviously, Gideon had been visiting someone who lived here on the fourth floor. That was worth looking into.

He set aside his camera and reached out to start his car. There was no need to follow the brothers anymore today. Tomorrow, he'd take the requisite photos of the wedding party entering and leaving the church.

Karen Lail

But his fellow paparazzi would look for him at the reception site in vain.

He would be *here*, staking out this apartment building, in the hope that Gideon would lead him to the person who lived here.

In the hope of an exclusive.

CHAPTER 16

Saturday, November 16ᵗʰ

Gideon and Gareth followed the preacher through the side door into the sanctuary. The brothers exchanged a look as they assumed their positions. Gareth was remarkably calm and self-assured. *He really is ready for this.*

Gideon surveyed the groom's side of the church. There was Mallory in the second pew with Courtney, Shannon, Avery, and Lettie. They shared a smile, and then he shifted his eyes to Graham and Garrison, who were approaching the front pew, Graham cradling a bouquet of flowers. Graham gently placed the flowers on the pew where his mother would have sat, and then headed back up the aisle. Garrison's jaw was tight with emotion as he entered the pew. He turned to sit down and met Gideon's gaze.

She's here with us, Dad.

Garrison gave a slight nod, as if he'd heard Gideon's thought.

Gideon pulled himself back to the moment, realizing Gabriel had just seated Rachel's mother and was walking back up the aisle. The organist transitioned into "Jesu, Joy of Man's Desiring." Gareth glanced at Gideon and stood a little straighter.

Ethan, Graham, and Gabriel filed down the aisle and lined up in their appointed places. One by one, the bridesmaids glided to their positions opposite the men. After a moment, Jesse and David moved slowly to the front, solemnly carrying the small rustic wood boxes Rachel had chosen instead of the traditional ring bearer pillows. Gideon winked at them as they stopped just in front of Gabriel.

When Meghan—Rachel's sister and maid of honor—reached the front of the church, the organist paused and then launched into Pachelbel's "Canon in D". Rachel's mother rose, and the rest of the congregation followed suit.

Gideon heard Gareth's intake of breath when Rachel and her father appeared. Gareth descended the three steps to meet them, shook her father's hand, and waited while her father kissed his daughter and placed her hand in Gareth's. Rachel passed her bouquet to Meghan and then held up the skirt of her dress with her left hand as Gareth tucked her right hand under his arm. The look of reverence on Gareth's face as he led his bride up to the altar brought tears to Gideon's eyes.

A sense of unreality settled over him as the ceremony began. This was it: his little brother—his playmate, his ally, his special charge—was getting married. And while it was right that a man should leave his family and be united to his wife as one flesh, it was hard on those left behind. He cut his eyes to his dad, who was holding the bouquet and wistfully stroking one of the petals as Gareth and Rachel recited their vows.

On cue, Gideon bent down to remove the rings from the boxes Jesse and David held out to him. *The next time Gareth comes to the house, it will be as a visitor. Unless...* He stole a glance at Mallory before removing the final ring. *I'll think about that later.* He straightened up, handed over the rings, and stepped back into position.

He enthusiastically led the applause when the pastor presented Mr. and Mrs. Gareth Locke to the congregation. Pausing while Meghan handed the bouquet back to Rachel and then adjusted the train of her dress, Rachel and Gareth walked joyfully up the aisle and stopped just outside the sanctuary doors. In lieu of a formal receiving line with their parents and attendants, they had opted to greet their guests alone.

Seeing that Meghan and the bridesmaids had been claimed by their respective spouses or dates, Gideon looked at his brothers and Ethan and signaled them with a quick sideways tilt of his head. They walked to the second pew and escorted the girls through the side door and into the church parlor, where they would wait with the rest of the wedding party until it was time for the post-ceremony photos.

Gideon drew Mallory into a corner of the room, away from the others. "I have to warn you: Rachel and Gareth want you and Ethan and Lettie to be in some of the photos with our family."

"Oh. Do I have to?"

"I know it will be hard for you, but I think it would hurt their feelings if you didn't."

He watched the emotions flickering across her face: consternation, hesitation, resignation. He took her hands in his. "I will be right beside you in every one. Besides," he said with a smile, "it will be nice to have a reminder of how fabulous we looked today. You really are lovely."

"Thank you," she replied with an embarrassed smile.

"So you'll do it?"

"Yes. We don't want any hurt feelings today."

"The limos are here and the shuttle is five minutes out," the wedding coordinator announced. Even though the hotel where the reception would be held was just fifteen minutes from the church, Rachel had arranged for a shuttle to transport the wedding party from the hotel, where they'd been instructed to leave their cars, to the church and back.

"Okay, thank you," Gareth answered.

"I'll go join the paparazzi outside," the wedding photographer said, slinging his camera bag over one shoulder and heading out the door.

Gareth looked at Rachel. "Ready?"

She nodded, looking around for her parents and her sister.

Jesse and David ran up to Gideon. "'Bye, Uncle Gideon," Jesse cried.

He stooped down and gave them each a high five. "'Bye, guys. You did great today! Be good for Avery's grandmother tonight, okay?"

"We will!" they chorused.

He watched with a grin as the boys ran off and then he stood up. "I'll see you there," he said, giving Mallory a quick peck.

"Lettie and I will look after her," Ethan promised before they went their separate ways—Gideon joining Rachel, Gareth, their parents, and Meghan in the vestibule at the front of the church; Ethan, Lettie, and Mallory falling into line with the rest of the group as they walked to the rear entrance.

Meghan twitched the back of Rachel's dress into place and straightened up. "All set."

"Here we go." Gideon said, holding the door open for the others to pass through.

Rachel and Gareth emerged first. They smiled and waved for the cameras, shared a brief kiss, and then entered the lead limousine. Rachel's parents, Garrison, Meghan, Gideon, and the photographer entered the second limo and then both cars pulled through the portico. As their limo turned left out of the front parking lot, Gideon saw the shuttle turning into the back lot. *I hope the paparazzi are too busy following us to care about the rest of the group.*

He had fulfilled his reception duties as best man.

Circulating around the ballroom to speak to the guests at each table.

Offering the first toast.

Dancing the obligatory dances: first with Meghan; then each bridesmaid; Rachel's mom; Rachel herself.

Scrambling with the other single men to catch the garter.

And now, finally, he was able to claim Mallory for the rest of the evening.

"I am really enjoying Gareth and Rachel's playlist," she said as they moved in time to Nat King Cole's version of "Stardust."

He nodded. "They both love to watch classic movies, so it was only natural that they chose songs from the 1940s, '50s, and '60s." He pulled her a little closer. "You know, dancing with you like this—here, in this ballroom, with me in my tux and you in your gown—well, now I have an idea what it would have felt like to go to prom."

She smiled up at him. "Trust me, this is much better than a prom." At his quizzical look, she explained: "No curfew, no teenage drama…"

"No chaperones," he chimed in, kissing her.

Gideon followed Ethan around to the passenger side of Ethan's car and opened the back door. As he helped Mallory out of the back seat, he suddenly felt uneasy. He scanned the parking lot of the apartment building and saw a man emerging from a car parked in the row behind them. The man's eyes met Gideon's briefly and then looked away as he walked past them towards the building, a messenger-style bag slung across his body and resting against his right hip.

Maybe it was a false alarm.

Ethan's car chirped twice as he pressed the Lock button on the key fob. Hand-in-hand, Gideon and Mallory fell into step behind Ethan and Lettie as they followed the sidewalk to the front of the building.

The man was holding open the door for them.

"Looks like you've been somewhere special," he remarked as he trailed them to the elevator.

"A wedding," Ethan replied, pressing the call button.

"Oh, nice."

They stepped onto the elevator and Gideon pressed the button for the fourth floor.

"Five, please," the man said, moving behind Mallory to the back right corner of the car, and Gideon pressed that button, too.

Noticing the man gazing intently at Mallory, Ethan's eyes met Gideon's and then cut to the man and back. Gideon angled himself between the man and Mallory while Ethan took a step back.

They were all silent as the elevator rose. The doors parted at the fourth floor, and the two couples stepped off, taking the zig-zag to the left that led to the girls' apartment.

Gideon heard the elevator doors close, and the tension drained from him, leaving him momentarily lightheaded.

Mallory turned to face him as Lettie unlocked the door to the apartment. "Are you all right?"

"Yes, I'm fine," he answered, giving her a kiss.

Drawing apart slightly, he saw that Mallory's eyes had widened in shock. Gideon looked over his shoulder, his fears realized.

The camera whirred rapidly.

Gideon got out of the car, closed the door, glanced swiftly around, and then slapped the roof of the car twice. Ethan put the car in gear and accelerated away from the curb, braking for the turn at the end of the street. Gideon listened for the reassuring snap of the gate closing behind him. Shouldering the garment bag that held Gareth's tux and shoes, he moved quickly into the shadows of the trees lining the driveway and circled around the garage. He entered the house through the back door and turned the deadbolt behind him.

He made his way through the house and up the stairs in darkness. Tugging at his bow tie, he entered his bedroom, cast the garment bag on his bed, and then sank onto the armchair by the window.

He was back to being a fugitive.

CHAPTER 17

Monday, November 18ᵗʰ

"She feels like a fugitive," Lettie told Gideon frankly as they walked up the steps to the library. "She dreads leaving the apartment."

Gideon smoothed the back of his hair. *I know that feeling.* He'd been tempted to wear his wig today, but had decided against it. If his relationship with Mallory was about to be made public, he wanted to make it clear that he was proud to be seen with her. "Has that photographer or anyone else been hanging around?"

"Not that we've seen."

"Odds are, then, that he's the only one who's found out about her so far. He's probably working with a reporter or investigator, trying to run down her name and any other information he can dig up on her before submitting the pictures."

"And what he can't find out, he'll invent," Lettie said cynically, leading the way into the library.

"Hopefully not."

She tossed him a skeptical look.

"I'm sorry, Lettie. I know this is hard on you, too."

"I can handle it. It's Mallory I'm worried about. I haven't seen her like this since—" She broke off. "Wait here. I'll find out where she is."

Gideon watched as she walked to the circulation desk and spoke to an older woman. Lettie turned and motioned him to follow her to the elevator.

They found Mallory seated on the floor among the stacks, reshelving the last remaining books from the rolling cart. Catching sight of them, she wearily got to her feet.

My God, he thought when he saw the pallor of her skin, the dark shadows under her eyes. "I know you're working," he said quietly, "but when you didn't answer my calls or texts yesterday, I just had to see you."

Her face crumpled. With a stifled sob, she cast herself into his arms. He held her close, soothing her as she softly wept.

Lettie laid one hand on Gideon's arm and caressed her cousin's back with the other, and then, with a nod to Gideon, she left them alone.

Mallory stepped back and wiped her eyes. "I'm sorry."

"I'm the one who's sorry, Mallory. I've been going over and over everything that went down Saturday night, and this I know: That photographer was already there in the parking lot, waiting for us," he murmured. "That means that at some point I got careless and led him straight to you. I was as shocked as you were. I guess I took it for granted that the media would be focused only on Gareth and Rachel."

"Rachel had warned me it would happen, but I guess part of me didn't believe it," she answered softly.

He nodded and dropped his voice to a whisper. "Unfortunately, as long as my brothers and I are in show business, this is what our lives will be like. And it's not just us—it bleeds over to our friends and family. So there's something you need to decide: Is our relationship worth the aggravation of being plagued by the media?" He held up his hand when she started to reply. "Don't answer me now. This is just *one* photographer… a very small tip of a very large iceberg. Wait until the word gets out and you really start getting hounded by paparazzi. Trust me, Mallory, it *will* happen. And when it does… well, I'll understand if you want to walk away, but," he pulled her to him in a tight hug, "I *hope* you won't."

She held the embrace a moment longer and then, suddenly aware of the curious glances from the students who were studying nearby, drew away. "I should get back to work—I have two more carts of books to restock before I leave."

"I understand." He searched her face. "Are you still up for dinner and a movie at my house?"

She looked down for one moment, two moments, three…

God, is she going to refuse?

"Okay," she said at last, raising her eyes to his.

Thank you, God.

"Good. I'll meet you at the circulation desk in forty-five minutes."

His source had said the girl—Mallory Glencoe, age 27, from some Podunk town in upstate New York—would be getting off work at five o'clock. He was taking a chance, sitting here near the main entrance of the library. There was always the possibility that she would leave by a different exit. But not too long ago he'd seen Gideon Locke go in through this very entrance, so odds were good that they would both leave this way.

He glanced at his watch. Any time now. He double-checked the settings on his camera and settled back to watch the people entering and exiting the library.

There! He swung up his camera and tracked Mallory and Gideon as they walked hand-in-hand down the library steps. The camera snapped rapidly, sending each image to the photographer's cloud drive.

The photographer placed his camera on the passenger seat, reached for his phone, and reviewed the photos he'd just taken. He selected the best ones and typed a text message.

> These should convince you that Gideon and the girl are still seeing each other. If I find out any other information about her, I'll forward it to you. As always, it's a pleasure doing business with you.

Verifying the photos were attached, he pressed Send.

"I'm so glad you agreed to have dinner with us," Garrison told Mallory. He and Gideon were seated on either side of her at the kitchen island, where they had decided to eat their informal meal.

"Thank you for having me. Everything is delicious," she said before taking another bite of her fajita.

"Gideon showed me the garage apartment plan you created for your class. I was really impressed."

She held up a finger as she finished chewing and then swallowed. "I was hoping you would like it."

"I don't know if I told you, but Gareth and Rachel are planning on living in the casita behind her parents' house temporarily," Gideon said. "They're not sure where they want to make their long-term home, so rather than rush into a decision, her parents offered to let them stay there for the time being."

"And while the casita gives them privacy, it really isn't much more than a guest room."

"Well, there *is* a kitchenette, but it just has a bar sink, a small refrigerator, and a microwave—there's no cooktop or oven, so there's no way to cook an actual meal. There's no laundry hook-up either, so they have to either use her parents' washer and dryer or go to a laundromat."

Garrison set down his fork and laid his arms on the counter. "So what Gideon was thinking, Mallory, is that we could use your plan to build that garage apartment for Gareth and Rachel. That way, instead of being confined to a space the size of a hotel room, they'd have room to cook, entertain, and spread out. They'd still have their privacy, they can live there as long as they want—and they would be completely self-sufficient."

"Courtney's father is a general contractor," Gideon interposed. "Dad showed him the design during the reception last night."

"He's agreed to take on the job and has even given me a ballpark figure. Our goal would be to start construction by the first week of January."

"Oh, wow. Garrison, that sounds wonderful. I'm thrilled that you like the plan well enough to want to build it. But I have to tell you: while I completed my practicum and became licensed in New York State before I started my master's program, I am not licensed in California. A California-licensed architect would have to make sure the plan meets any state or local code requirements."

"But if you turned your design over to another architect for sign off, wouldn't the plans basically become their property?" Gideon asked.

"Not necessarily. I have proof of the date I submitted the design to my professor. In fact, Dr. Ames *is* licensed in California, so maybe he would be willing to collaborate with me on the actual drawings that would have to be submitted to the county." She looked at Garrison. "If you're serious about wanting to start construction in January, I can email him tonight or tomorrow to see if he could meet with us in the next few days to talk about it."

"Could you email him now? My schedule is wide open the rest of this week, if that works for him. I'm really anxious to get things lined up for this so that we can surprise Gareth and Rachel with the idea when they get back from their honeymoon."

Mallory pulled out her phone and typed a quick message.

> Hi, Dr. Ames. I showed my Year 2175 design to the property owner. He's interested in building that addition. He has already lined up a general contractor and would like to begin construction in January. I explained that I'm not licensed in California but wondered if you would be willing to collaborate on the plans? Let me know if you would be interested. The property owner would be willing to meet this week whenever it suits you. Thank you!

"Okay. Hopefully I'll hear from him before long," she said, laying her phone down next to her plate.

Her phone dinged as they were clearing the dishes. Garrison and Gideon waited expectantly as Mallory picked it up.

"It's Dr. Ames." She scanned the email response. "He can meet Thursday evening at six-thirty. He wants to know if we could meet *here* so that he could see the garage in person."

"Are you free at that time, too?" Garrison asked.

"Yes, I can make it work."

"Then go ahead and give him my address, and lock it down for Thursday."

Mallory keyed the information and sent it. A moment later, the phone dinged again. "We're all set."

CHAPTER 18

Thursday, November 21ˢᵗ

D r. Frederick Ames made a notation on his tablet. "I get the same measurements. Your design will work very nicely with this space, Mallory. It not only blends with the garage, but complements the main house as well. And you're right—we'll probably need at least one lam beam running the length of the two-car section, and some sort of reinforcement to support the weight of the kitchen island. We may need another lam beam to support the ceiling and roof over the living and dining room."

"Lam beam?" Garrison asked.

"Short for laminated beam," Dr. Ames replied. "Basically, it's several long boards that are adhered together to form a beam. They give support and stability to the structure above. Once we open up the ceiling of the garage, we'll know better what we're working with. I'll have the structural engineer at my firm take a look when we reach that point." He grinned at Mallory. "Congratulations, Mallory. You've earned an A on this project."

"Thank you!"

He looked at Garrison. "Now we just have to settle on materials. One concern I have is whether we will be able to match some of the exterior building products."

"Yes, Dan Spaulding—the general contractor who will be working on the project—was worried about that as well. He's going to source some options for us."

"Good. I've worked with Dan in the past—he's top-notch. Well, all that's left is for Mallory to tell us what she used for the interior finishes, and if you'd like something different, we can make a note of that."

"You mean choosing colors and things?"

"No, just the *types* of finishes: quartz countertops versus granite or some other stone, hardwood floors versus luxury vinyl, porcelain tile or ceramic… things like that," Mallory explained.

"So Gareth and Rachel will be able to have a say in the actual colors, right?" Gideon asked.

"Absolutely."

"Oh, good to know. Well, why don't we go inside where we can be more comfortable," Garrison invited.

Gideon's phone rang as they entered through the kitchen and headed towards the living room. He glanced at the caller ID. "Excuse me while I take this." He accepted the call and placed the phone against his ear as he walked back into the kitchen. "Hi, Ethan. What's up?"

"Are you at home?"

"Yes. Why?"

"You need to turn on the TV and watch the report Caitlyn Snow will be airing after the commercial break. I think it's going to be about you and Mallory!"

Oh great. He moved into the family room. "What channel?… Okay, I'll have to DVR it and watch it later. Thanks for the heads up, Ethan."

"No problem. Take care."

Gideon picked up the TV remote and pointed it at the television. *This just may drive her back into her shell.*

Unless…

For a moment, he considered hiding the truth; pretending Ethan had called about another matter.

No. This news report would probably open the floodgates of publicity, so better that she be prepared, not blindsided, when other photographers and reporters started showing up.

With a few clicks of the remote buttons, he started recording the celebrity news show, then tossed the remote onto the sofa and headed to the living room.

Mallory looked up at him with a smile when he entered, then did a double-take, her smile fading. "Is something wrong?" she whispered as he sat beside her on the love seat.

"Just a message from Ethan. I'll show you later."

Dr. Ames drew her attention. "So Mallory, what did you have in mind for the finishes?"

"Well, I was trying to go with things that are timeless, not necessarily on trend. For durability, I was thinking we could use wood-look porcelain tile throughout, but I know that would require extra support for the floor, which translates into more costs…"

Gideon nodded when expected but his thoughts kept straying to two questions.

What would be in Caitlyn Snow's report?
And how would Mallory react?

As they rolled up to the stoplight, Gideon reached over, took hold of her hand, and broke the heavy silence that had settled between them ever since saying goodbye to Garrison.

"I guess that report keeps replaying in your mind like it is in mine."

She glanced at him and nodded wordlessly before resuming her sightless stare out the window. Caitlyn Snow's words had been looping without ceasing ever since she and Gideon had watched the segment:

> For several weeks now, rumors have been circulating on social media that Gideon Locke has begun dating again. Those rumors were confirmed this weekend following the wedding of his brother Gareth to the former Rachel Manning. Sources say that his new love is Mallory Glencoe, a 27-year-old master's candidate at the Talbot C. Pollard Institute for Industrial, Architectural, and Interior Design. Ms. Glencoe is a native of Hepton Grove, a small town in upstate New York. She is reportedly the first person Gideon has dated since his breakup with actress Trish Galloway last year.

"It was a shock hearing all that they've found out about me. I keep wondering who the 'sources' are," she said as the light changed.

"I know it's hard, but you've got to stop worrying about that. The sources may not be actual *people*—there are so many databases they can tap into now."

"True."

"I'm just glad it was Caitlyn Snow who broke the story rather than one of the tabloids. At least she seems to be concerned with getting the facts right."

"So there will be others who *won't* care about getting it right?"

"I'm afraid so." He made the turn into the apartment parking lot and pulled into a space. He switched off the car and turned slightly to face her. "So let me give you the same advice that Kendra gave us years ago. Try not to look at the tabloids and magazines when you're checking out at a grocery store or passing a newsstand. If you're suddenly faced with a crowd of reporters, hold your head up and just keep walking past them. Don't stop, don't answer them, and if possible, don't make eye contact with them, no matter what they do or say—and believe me, they'll do whatever they can to get a reaction from you. If they ask you for an interview, refer them to Ethan's mom. Okay?"

"Okay."

He unbuckled his seat belt and reached for his key fob.

She placed a restraining hand on his arm. "You don't need to walk me up."

"Yes," he replied. "I do. And I intend to spend every possible minute with you between now and when I leave for Branson, if you let me. Deal?"

Laughing, she grasped his outstretched hand. "Deal."

CHAPTER 19

Tuesday, November 26th

Mallory likened them to the plague of locusts. They swarmed around her as she exited the apartment building shortly after 7:00 a.m. and walked to the bus stop. They trailed her to campus, surrounding her as she stepped off the city bus. They fed on her every move, every expression, and, still not satisfied, clamored for more.

"Where did you and Gideon meet?"

"How long have you been dating?"

"Is it true you're traveling to Branson with him?"

"Do you think your relationship will last longer than all the others he's had?"

Bewildered by the barrage of questions and the continued targeting of the cameras, she couldn't move, couldn't think.

And then the bell tower chimed the quarter hour, startling her into action.

"Please, I need to get to class!" she cried, trying to sidle her way through the crowd.

A photographer stepped directly in front of her, blocking her path as he snapped a picture.

"Please," she repeated more loudly, causing several students nearby to look at her curiously.

The photographer smirked, gave a mock salute, and retreated.

Once past the throng of paparazzi, she fought the temptation to run. Thankful that she was wearing her white Keds today, she set a brisk pace across the quadrangle and entered a building through the automatic door. She paused, noting that the elevator light indicated the elevator was rising to the third floor. She turned and dashed up the stairs to her classroom.

Safe, she thought gratefully as she slipped into her seat.

"Mallory," the raven-haired girl beside her whispered.

"What?"

"There's a guy out front who's been offering money for pictures of you. *I* told him to get lost, but there may be some students who are desperate enough to take him up on it. I just thought you should know."

"Thanks, Sofia."

Her hands shaking, she pulled out her phone and started a text to Gideon. Catching sight of Sofia's hoodie, she broke off in mid-sentence. *It had worked once. Would it work again?*

Immediately after class, she headed to the campus bookstore. Taking the white and green plastic bag from the cashier, she stuffed her purchase out of sight in her laptop bag and headed to the library.

"Mallory, what are you doing here? You're not scheduled to work today," the shift supervisor said as Mallory approached the circulation desk.

"Hi, Mrs. Carlyle. I just came by to pick up something that I left here the other day."

"Oh, okay. Well, enjoy your Thanksgiving break."

"You too."

Mallory passed through the door marked Staff Only.

A green headband hanging around her neck, she was pulling her hair into a ponytail when Gideon's text showed up on her phone.

Out front. Courtney's van.

She texted a reply, tucked her phone away and zipped her laptop tote, and then tilted the tote sideways and slid it inside the green track pants she had donned over her jeans. The bulk of the bag filled out the men's size medium pants as she'd hoped. A couple of folds of the waistband drew up enough of the length that she could walk comfortably. She zipped up the matching jacket, pushed up the sleeves slightly, and then pulled the headband up in place and slipped on her dark-framed glasses. She picked up the price tags she'd removed from the track suit and tossed them into the trashcan, and then studied her reflection. She folded her left arm across her body, holding the tote in place. Parting her lips, she exhaled, her breath rebounding off the surface of the mirror; then she turned, pulled open the restroom door, emerged from the Staff Only area, strode past Mrs. Carlyle and the circulation desk, and exited the library.

Courtney's van was idling at the curb. Mallory skipped down the library steps, saw Gideon sitting behind the wheel, and got in.

As soon as the door closed, Gideon glanced over his shoulder and accelerated away from the curb. Meanwhile, Mallory hastily unzipped her jacket and tugged her tote bag free, depositing it on the floorboard before fastening her seat belt.

"That was a clever way to disguise your figure," he grinned as he guided the van into the left turning lane, braking for the stoplight. "Super Designer Woman strikes again."

Mallory smiled wanly and, sighing, turned her head to look out her window.

He stretched out his hand and laid it on Mallory's. "Are you okay?"

Mallory laced her fingers through his, her eyes focused on the slightly smaller crowd of paparazzi that still loitered at the main entrance to the campus. "I am now." She turned in her seat and looked at him. "Thank you for rescuing me."

"My pleasure."

She scanned the rest of the van's interior. "Where are Courtney and the boys?"

"They've gone with Gabriel to pick up lunch for everybody," he replied. The light changed, and Gideon made the turn. "Do you need to go back to your apartment for anything before we head to my house?"

"No, but there's another stop I'd like to make on the way, if you don't mind. But first," she said, leaning down to unzip each leg of the track pants, "I'm going to get out of this outfit." She shrugged out of the pants, folded them neatly, and then removed and folded the jacket as well. She then placed the outfit on the console between them. "Consider this part of your Christmas present," she said with a smile.

Laughing, he kissed the back of her hand.

"It's so good to see you!" Mallory exclaimed, hugging Rachel and Gareth in turn as she and Gideon entered through the kitchen door.

"Thanks. We had a great time, but it's good to be home," Gareth responded. Rachel nodded her agreement as she drew away from Gideon's brotherly hug.

"I'm going to run this upstairs," Gideon said, gesturing to the track suit. "Be right back."

Garrison appeared in the doorway from the family room. "Is that what I think it is?" he asked, gesturing to the cardboard tube in Mallory's left hand.

"It sure is," she replied, crossing over to hand it to him. "I had the printer make eight sets for you—that should be more than enough."

"I can't believe you got them done so quickly. Thank you so much!"

"You're welcome!"

"What is it? Eight sets of what?" asked Gareth.

"We'll show you later," Garrison promised, placing the tube on top of the refrigerator.

"Pizza's here!" Gabriel sang out as he and Graham, each carrying two large boxes, entered with their respective families.

Gareth stopped and inhaled deeply, a beatific smile spreading across his face. "That smells amazing! The food in Hawaii was great, but I've been craving some good pizza."

Rachel laughed up at him and pulled him forward to greet the rest of the family. "Me too!"

Minutes later, seated around the dining table under the pergola, Garrison called everyone to order. "This time together is to celebrate the safe return of Gareth and Rachel from their honeymoon." He lifted his glass to them. "Welcome home."

"Welcome home!" the others repeated with cheers and claps.

"We're glad to be back," Gareth said with a smile.

"It's also the last meal we'll be able to share with Mallory until January," he continued. "By the time we get back from Branson, the fall semester will be over and Mallory will already be in New York for Christmas." He looked at her. "We'll miss you."

The rest of the family echoed the sentiment.

Fighting back sudden tears, Mallory looked around at each of them, her gaze finally resting on Gideon. "I will miss you, too."

"But let's not be sad—this is the season of thankfulness and joy and hope and love. So after we eat, let's decorate for Christmas. And we'll look forward to the time when we're all together again," Garrison ended, his voice breaking a little.

Gideon and Gareth exchanged a poignant look across the table. *Dad's thinking about Mom.*

"Can I help, too, Grandpa?" Jesse asked. "And can we sing Christmas songs after?"

"Me too! Me too!" David exclaimed.

"You sure can. I wouldn't have it any other way."

"Yay!" the boys chorused as baby Avery clapped her hands.

———

They decided to divide and conquer. Graham, Gideon, and Gareth pulled out a couple of ladders and hung strands of lights on the front of the house and garage. Garrison and Gabriel, together with Jesse and David, set up the Balsam Hill tree and began decorating it as Avery looked on from her play yard. Shannon draped artificial pine garland in graceful swags down the length of the banister. Courtney volunteered to freshen and hang the wreaths in the family room, kitchen, and on the front door. Rachel and Mallory were tasked with decorating the main living spaces with an assortment of candles, greenery, and seasonal items.

In the foyer, Mallory laid the last of the pine cones in the small apothecary jar on the console table and replaced the lid. She stepped back to study the tablescape, then turned the vase of red and white silk flowers slightly and adjusted the greenery around the base.

She looked up as Courtney approached, carrying a wreath and its metal hanger.

"That wreath is beautiful," Mallory said, taking the wreath hanger from her and opening the front door. She placed the hanger over the door.

"It is, isn't it?" Courtney agreed as she carefully hung and centered the wreath. "Grace made it—she was so talented that way." She closed the front door and surveyed the foyer and stairway with satisfaction. "It looks so pretty in here. I'm *so* glad Garrison wanted to do this. It's a good sign."

Mallory nodded.

"Is there anything you and Rachel need help with?" asked Courtney.

"No, I think this was the last thing we were going to do."

"Then let's go see how the tree is coming, shall we? If I know Jesse and David, they've hung their ornaments all in a cluster at their eye level. It'll take some coaxing to get them to spread them out."

Graham, Gideon, and Gareth walked in moments later and joined the others around the Christmas tree.

"I think we need to take a group picture," Garrison remarked, looking archly at Shannon.

"I'm on it, Garrison," she answered with a chuckle. In just minutes she had set up her camera, positioned everyone, adjusted the focus, and set the timer before slipping into place next to Graham, who held Avery with one arm.

Gideon noticed Mallory's head was bent forward. He was about to whisper something encouraging to her, when she suddenly raised her head just moments before the flash flared.

Something niggled at the back of Gideon's mind and then was gone.

"Let's take a couple more," Shannon said, moving forward to set up for the next shot.

"Yay!" Jesse exclaimed when the last picture had been snapped. "Let's sing now!"

"Us first! Us first!" David cried.

"'Nounce us, Grandpa!" Jesse urged, pulling David back behind the tree with him.

"And now, ladies and gentlemen, singing 'Jingle Bells,' here are Jesse and David Locke!" Garrison said grandly, sweeping one arm towards the tree.

There was a burst of applause as Jesse and David bounded out from behind the branches, waving to everyone as they had seen their father and uncles do countless times. While the others laughed at the boys' posturing, Gabriel caught and held Courtney's troubled gaze.

"Mommy, Daddy, watch!" said Jesse imperiously.

"We're watching," Gabriel answered as he and Courtney turned and smiled at their sons.

Pretending to hold microphones in front of their mouths, they launched into the chorus.

Gareth and Rachel gave Shannon, Graham, and Avery a farewell hug and watched as they headed to their car. Gabriel and his family were already easing down the driveway in Courtney's minivan. With a final wave, Gareth closed the front door and, lacing his fingers with Rachel's, walked with her back to the kitchen where Garrison was smoothing out a set of bound blueprints on the kitchen island. Gideon brought over salt and pepper shakers and placed them on diagonal corners of the blueprint pages.

Curious, Gareth and Rachel joined Garrison, Gideon, and Mallory at the island and peered at the topmost page, which was a front elevation of the garage.

"'Locke Garage Addition'," Gareth read aloud.

Rachel looked at Mallory. "So *this* is your project—the one Gideon and Garrison helped take all those measurements for?"

Mallory nodded.

"I thought you said you weren't going to use our name," Rachel said.

Gareth gave her a quick kiss and smiled down at her. "'Our name'—I love it when you say that."

Mallory started to reply to Rachel, but Garrison intervened.

"Mallory sent me the screen shots of what she submitted to her professor, and she *didn't* use our name on those," he stated. "What we have here," he said, gesturing to the blueprints, "are the formal plans for the apartment we're going to build for the two of you."

Rachel and Gareth looked at each other in surprise. "What?" they cried in unison.

"I don't understand," Gareth continued.

"Gideon suggested we use Mallory's design to build this apartment for you."

"Of course, if you'd rather stay in the casita, I'll be glad to take it in your place," Gideon teased.

"I've already talked to Courtney's dad, and he is ready to start on it in January."

"Wow, I don't know what to say." Gareth looked at Rachel questioningly.

"Can we see the floorplan?" she asked Garrison.

"Sure. It's your design, Mallory, so why don't walk them through it?"

"All right."

Gideon and Garrison each picked up a shaker and Mallory turned the page.

"Oh no," Mallory moaned as she and Gideon turned into the parking lot of her apartment building. "I was hoping no one would be here."

Gideon shifted the SUV into park and looked over at her. "I'm afraid they'll be hanging around for the next couple of weeks."

"Even after you leave for Branson tomorrow?"

He nodded. "Probably right up until the day you fly home to New York."

She buried her face in her hands for a moment.

Gideon gently tucked a lock of hair behind her ear. "I'm sorry."

She raised her head and studied him by the light of the streetlamp for a moment, and then leaned forward and kissed him.

He drew back and smiled at her, tracing her cheek with one finger. "Ready to face them?"

"I guess so."

"It's like I told you: hold your head up and just keep walking." He opened his door. "Just stay there. I'm coming around for you."

The photographers rushed at them, jockeying for position as Gideon walked around and opened Mallory's door. Momentarily disoriented by the rapid flashes, she dipped her head and clung tightly to his hand as he helped her out of the car. She was trembling when he slipped his arm around her, and he held her close, ignoring the questions that were being hurled at them, his focus only on Mallory. He felt her take a breath, and then she raised her head, met his eyes briefly before looking straight ahead, letting him guide her past the photographers and into the building. He pushed the elevator call button, and the doors parted.

"You did great," he said as soon as the doors closed behind them.

"I'm so glad you were with me."

Mallory saw Lettie's note on the console table, and she held it so that she and Gideon could read it together.

> Ethan and I have gone to the store to pick up some snacks for us. Back soon. Don't start the movie without us!!!
>
> P.S. – Your mail is on the kitchen island.

"It was nice of them to give us a few minutes of privacy," Gideon said with a grin as he slipped his arms around her.

She smiled and put her arms around his neck, lifting her face for his kiss.

"I'm going to miss you so much," he said softly, holding her close to him.

"I'm going to miss you too."

The ringing of Mallory's phone interrupted them.

She glanced at the caller ID. "It's Max," she told Gideon. "I'll be right back. Go ahead and get something to drink."

"Okay. What would you like?"

"Water, please." She spun and headed for her bedroom. "Hi, Max."

Gideon got out two glasses and pulled the water pitcher from the refrigerator. As he started to fill the glasses, he noticed the handwritten card lying on top of the small pile of mail. The name at the bottom caught his eye and, despising himself, he scanned the message.

Mallory,

I'm sorry I missed you again. Your part-time career with us is just a phone call away. Please contact me at your earliest convenience so that we can discuss your contract. I look forward to our association.

Regards,

Marcus Webber

"Marcus Webber!" he cried, his heart plummeting. *Trish's Marcus.*

He looked at the last sentence again: "I look forward to our association."

How could it be possible? Mallory was terrified of having her picture taken.

But wait... He remembered when they were posing for the group picture around the tree. Mallory had been looking down and then had suddenly raised her head and smiled. There had been something about that move that seemed familiar...

And then he remembered: It was one of the tricks the photographer for their first album had taught them—a way of giving a more natural-looking smile for the camera.

He placed both hands flat on the island. *No, God, please! Not Mallory too!*

He was leaning against the counter, his head bowed, when Mallory returned to the kitchen.

"Max said there are reporters and photographers hanging around our house and the clinic. I gave him the same advice you gave me." She looked at him curiously when he didn't answer. "Gideon, is something wrong?"

He raised his head and suddenly she felt she was reliving that moment when Gideon had first seen her in the suite at the football game—he had the same look of suspicion but something else, too. *Scorn?*

He picked up the postcard and tossed it towards her. "You've been talking to *Marcus Webber* about a *contract* and you ask if anything is wrong?"

"You read my mail?"

"It was laying there for anyone to see. What's going on, Mallory? His note says he wants to put you under a part-time contract; that he's 'looking forward to your association'."

"Gideon, this is L.A. We get stuff like this from agencies all the time. It doesn't mean anything."

"Someone else told me that not so long ago and *she* ended up being one of his clients."

Her voice rose. "So now you're comparing me to *Trish Galloway*?" She tossed her head in vexation. "No, Gideon, I am *not* talking to Marcus Webber or *anyone* about a contract or an association or anything else. I'm an architect, and proud of it. I have *zero* interest in being an actress or a model or whatever it is Marcus Webber does. I thought *you* of all people knew that."

"I thought so too. *This* proves I was wrong," he retorted, pointing at the postcard.

He doesn't believe me. Even worse, he doesn't want *to believe me.* With heartsick clarity, her mind reeled back to January, and her first negative impressions of L.A… her conviction that she would never stay for more than two weeks in this city.

And suddenly, Mallory had had enough. Between the stress of being hounded by paparazzi, the growing dread she'd felt at having to say goodbye to Gideon, and now his baseless accusation of signing on with an agent, she was done.

She brushed away angry tears and took a steadying breath. "Thank you, Gideon. You've reminded me of something I've tried to ignore ever since I've met you: I want *nothing* to do with show business, or *anyone* who's involved in it. Not ever again," she said resolutely, spinning the postcard like a Frisbee and turning away. Startled, he grabbed for the card as it bounced off his chest. When he captured it, he looked up in time to see her enter her bedroom. The door snapped shut.

Exhaling deeply, Gideon headed towards the door to the apartment and saw Lettie and Ethan staring at him, shocked. "Sorry to ruin your evening," he said, wrenching the door open. He walked out without a backwards glance.

Garrison, seated at the kitchen island, looked up from his laptop when Gideon entered through the back door. "Were there many photographers at Mallory's apartment?"

"A few, but we just pushed past them."

"You didn't stay long. I thought you were planning on watching a movie or something."

He shrugged. "Our plans changed. Besides, I still have some packing to do. What are you up to?"

Garrison gestured to his laptop. "Just going over some numbers. Oh, and I received word that the backup band and your instruments arrived in Oklahoma City. They'll make the final leg to Branson tomorrow."

"Good. Well, goodnight, Dad."

"Gideon."

He turned to face his father.

"Is everything all right?"

Gideon forced his lips into a smile. "Nothing that time won't heal. Goodnight."

"'Night, son."

Gideon placed a stack of shirts in his open suitcase. As he started to turn back to his dresser, his gaze fell on the neatly folded track suit he'd placed on his bed earlier. He picked up the jacket and held it to his nose. Yes, there it was: the subtle fragrance that would inextricably be linked to his memories of her.

Still clutching the jacket, he sank into the armchair and stared mournfully out the window.

CHAPTER 20

Wednesday, November 27th

Dallas, TX

Lettie's text came while Gideon and his family were in the Dallas-Fort Worth airport, waiting for their connecting flight to Springfield, Missouri:

> I'm sorry about what happened to you and
> Mallory. I'm not trying to meddle—I just want
> to show you that she was telling the truth.

Her next message contained pictures of postcards and other mailers from various talent agencies. The last one was from Marcus Webber, a word-for-word duplicate of the postcard sent to Mallory, but addressed to Letitia.

He exited Lettie's text and looked at the photo he now used as his phone's wallpaper: one of the group shots of his family and Mallory around the Christmas tree.

"That's such a good picture," Graham commented as he settled next to Gideon. He pointed to Mallory's face. "That's quite a difference from the first pictures Shannon took of her. I guess those tips Shannon gave her really helped."

Gideon looked at his brother. "What did you say?"

"I said the tips Shannon gave Mallory really helped her. She doesn't have that deer-in-the-headlights look like she did the night we first met her."

"Daddy, Daddy!" Avery piped. Turning, Graham and Gideon saw Shannon and Avery returning hand-in-hand from the ladies' room, a diaper bag slung over one of Shannon's shoulders.

Grinning, Graham got up and swooped up his daughter, carrying her as he and Shannon resumed their seats next to Gabriel and his family.

Gideon studied his sister-in-law for a moment before turning and slumping in his seat. Closing his eyes, he recalled the night he'd first brought Mallory home.

The moment he'd entered the kitchen and found Shannon and Mallory talking privately.

Was that when Shannon had coached Mallory?

His phone still clutched in his hand, he sprang up from his seat and started pacing. Seeing Marcus Webber's postcard had been his worst nightmare come to life. But that's all it was… just a nebulous, unfounded illusion. *He* was the one who had mistakenly believed it was real.

Believed it over everything Mallory had said.

How could I have been such an idiot?

Suddenly, all he wanted was to call Mallory, apologize to her, beg her to forgive him, to give him another chance.

He looked at his phone. She probably won't answer my call. But maybe she'll listen to a message.

He considered the words he would speak that would compel her to listen to his entire apology. He urgently dialed Mallory's cell phone and waited for her voicemail greeting.

But after one brief ring, a robotic male voice relayed a different message: *Blocked.*

Stunned, he ended the call and stared at his phone before slowly putting it into his pocket. He moved to the window overlooking the tarmac.

Blocked.

If only there were a way to turn back the clock to last night, to make it play out as he'd envisioned: with an exchange of promises to stay in touch over the next few weeks, as their schedules allowed. A promise to look ahead to the new year, when they would be reunited. And, if his nerve didn't fail him, his declaration of love for her.

Instead, he'd lost it.

Lost it all.

CHAPTER 21

Monday, December 9th

Los Angeles, CA

Mallory sent the last email to her professor and leaned back in her chair. The semester was officially over now. Tomorrow at this time she and Lettie would be somewhere over the Midwest, heading to Philadelphia.

It can't come soon enough.

It had been almost two weeks since that disastrous blowup with Gideon. She couldn't deny it: She missed him. She loved him. She regretted losing her temper. But she was just one semester away from finishing her degree and returning to New York for good. Her path and Gideon's were diametrically opposed. So, while she was remorseful over the way she had broken up with him, it was better for both of them that they parted.

At least, that's what she told herself during the day, when she could rationalize her actions and rigidly govern her emotions. But at night, her dreams betrayed her. Dreams of what had been.

Worse still, dreams of what might have been.

And, invariably, she would wake up crying.

Mallory's phone dinged. *Rachel.* From the moment they'd met, she had felt a connection to Rachel; it was this connection that even now prevented her from severing her last tie to the Locke family. Although she and Rachel tacitly avoided the topic of Gideon, they kept each other up to date on other things.

Mallory looked at the picture message.

> It's snowing! We're all taking the kids to see
> Santa later today.

"I've got something to show you," Lettie said somberly from the open door of Mallory's bedroom.

Mallory exited Rachel's message and sighed heavily. "Don't tell me he sent another bouquet."

"No, it's not a peace offering from Gideon." She handed a paper to her. "A new article has hit. And it's bad, Mallory—I mean, *really* bad."

Alarmed, Mallory took the tabloid from her cousin and looked at the front page. The headline screamed, "Gideon's girlfriend beaten! Was he to blame?" And underneath the headline was one of the pictures taken by the campus security officers nearly three years earlier.

"Oh, no—no, no, *no!*"

"There's more inside."

Fingers stiff, she struggled to turn the pages.

The "article" was nothing more than a highly speculative paragraph, but the pictures were what drew the eye. There were two more photos that the security officers had taken at the infirmary. There was a picture of Jackson, with a caption identifying him as her "discarded fiancé." *Oh, please,* she scoffed to herself. There were pictures of Gideon leading her protectively to her apartment that last dreadful night they were together. And, finally, a photo of a grim-faced Gideon, exiting the apartment building alone.

She dropped the paper. "This is awful," she whispered, horrified.

"What can I do?" Lettie asked.

Mallory propped her head on her hands. "Give me a few minutes. I need to think!"

"Okay," she said soothingly before withdrawing.

Lettie was peeking out through the vertical blinds on the balcony door when Mallory joined her about fifteen minutes later.

"There are even more paparazzi out there than there were a few minutes ago. They're like buzzards circling a carcass."

"Oh, Lettie, please."

"I'm sorry." She faced her cousin. "So did you come up with something?"

"I think so. Can you get hold of Ethan's mom?"

"I sure can," she said, pulling out her phone and scrolling to Kendra's contact information. A moment later, she spoke into the phone.

"Hello, Kendra? I guess you've seen the latest article about Mallory and Gideon… Yes, that one. Do you mind if I put Mallory on the line? She has something she wants to talk over with you. Okay, thank you." She passed the phone to Mallory.

"Thanks so much for talking to me, Mrs. Thomas… Okay, *Kendra*. Lettie and I are flying home tomorrow, so we don't have much time, but I'm hoping you can help. This is what I was thinking…"

Lettie's phone rang about forty-five minutes later. "I've got you on speaker, Kendra."

"Good. I've made all the arrangements. I've booked a hotel suite in my name for you girls. You'll stay there tonight and leave for the airport from there. I know you won't be back until January, but this is important: *don't* take any luggage with you. Pack your TSA toiletries, your phone charger, and just a change of clothes in your book bag or computer bag. You need to make it look like you're just going to campus. If you don't normally carry a purse when you go to class, hide that in your bag as well. That way, the paparazzi will think you'll be returning to the apartment, and will be less likely to try to follow you. Got it?"

"Yes, we understand," Lettie said.

"Good. Now, a town car will be parked just down the street from your apartment in twenty minutes. The driver will ask for a name. Give him mine. He'll know where to take you. Ethan and I will meet you in the lobby to get you checked in, and then we'll go from there."

"Sounds good. Thank you, Kendra," said Lettie.

"Yes, thank you so much," Mallory echoed.

"My pleasure. See you shortly."

The elevator lowered them to the main floor.

"I'm not sure I'm ready for this," Lettie confessed.

Mallory parroted Gideon's words: "Hold your head up and just keep walking." She tightened her hold on her laptop tote and looked ahead resolutely. "If nothing else, I want them to see that I'm not bruised and battered now." She pushed open the door and led the way out of the building. Heads erect, together they walked the gantlet of photographers and reporters and turned towards the street.

The town car was parked just past the bus stop shelter. As they approached, the driver stepped out of the car.

"What's the name?" he asked.

"Kendra Thomas."

He gave a nod and, smiling, held open the passenger door.

Branson, MO

Gareth knocked urgently on Gideon's hotel room door. After a beat, the door opened and Gareth stepped inside.

"There's something you've got to see," he said, holding out his phone.

Gideon took it from him with one hand while he closed the door with the other. Seeing the headline, he sank down on one of the chairs and scrolled slowly down the web page.

"We've got to get hold of Kendra right away and have her say these pictures are fake," Gareth urged.

"But they're *not* fake," Gideon answered, still focused on the phone. *What you must have gone through, you poor girl.*

"*What?*" Gareth dropped into the other chair. "What happened?"

He handed the phone back to his brother. "I can't tell you, Gareth—I can't break a confidence. All you need to know is that it happened long before I met her."

"But we can't let this story go unchallenged! It's accusing *you* of doing this to her! You've *got* to have Kendra do something!"

Gideon reached for his phone. "First, I'm going to text Ethan and have him check on Mallory, and *then* I'll see what Kendra thinks."

I saw the article implying I beat up Mallory.
This is going to bring the paparazzi out in
droves. Can you check on her for me and make
sure she's okay?

Ethan's response came just seconds later. Mutely, Gideon showed it to Gareth.

Already on it. The girls are safely tucked away in
a hotel. We're working on a rebuttal. One of us
will be in touch later today.

"That's a relief."
Gideon gave a nod and typed:

Thanks. Tell your mom not to bill the LLC—I
will reimburse her personally for all the hotel
expenses. Don't let Mallory know!

He had just sent the message when a group text from Garrison appeared on both Gareth's and Gideon's phones:

Family meeting in 10 minutes. My room.

The brothers traded looks and stood up. "I guess we know what the topic is," Gideon said drily.

"Yeah. The good news is, it can't be a long meeting since Dad promised the kids we'd all have our picture taken with Santa before we have to get ready for the first performance."

The update about the rebuttal came from Kendra, not Ethan, when Gideon and his family were next in line to see Santa.

He read and reread the text, dismay expanding within him like a sponge.

His family moved forward. Gideon trailed after them, still studying his phone. *Why would she have done that?*

He pocketed his phone and looked up to see Santa watching him.

The same Santa who had been standing outside a Los Angeles jewelry store just over a year ago.

Santa looked down at the children and asked what they wanted for Christmas. The boys enthusiastically recited their wishes, while Avery waved and chattered.

The family posed for a couple of pictures with Santa, and then Santa handed each of them a candy cane. As the family started filing towards the exit, Santa held up a finger to stop Gideon. Gideon bent down so he and Santa could speak privately. After a few minutes, Gideon shook Santa's hand and moved away.

"What was that all about?" Gareth asked.

Gideon shrugged. "Just doing a little catching up." He glanced at the wall clock. There just might be time. He pulled out his phone. "You go ahead with the others. I'll be along in a moment."

CHAPTER 22

Wednesday, December 11ᵗʰ

Hepton Grove

Hair wrapped in a towel, Mallory tightened the belt of her bathrobe as she studied the contents of her closet.

Three sets of scrubs left over from working at the clinic. One pair of black jeans. Four long-sleeved muted plaid flannel shirts. Some dreary winter-weight dresses and skirts. Black and gray sweatshirts.

Sighing, she turned to her dresser and opened the three bottom drawers one at a time.

Long johns, tights, and leggings.

Black sweaters.

Gray sweaters.

She opted for the black jeans and a gray sweater. As she dressed and then dried her hair, she debated whether she would tell her family about Gideon. Yesterday's flight from Philadelphia had been delayed due to a mechanical problem, so it had been nearly six when she and Lettie had landed in Albany. Her parents, Uncle Donald, and Aunt Kaye had been waiting for them in Baggage Claim, and mom and Aunt Kaye had each brought a winter coat for the girls. As they shrugged into the coats, the girls lightheartedly described Monday's escape from the apartment. They ended the tale at the point of meeting Ethan and Kendra in the hotel lobby, downplaying all the tension they'd felt and completely omitting the events that had occurred after they had checked in.

When they'd reached the parking deck, Mallory realized why Max hadn't come to the airport, too: her parents had picked up Uncle Donald and Aunt Kaye on the way. As they all got into the Chevy Tahoe, Uncle Donald suggested they stop for dinner before heading up the Northway, so it was just after eight when they dropped Lettie and her parents off in Saratoga Springs. Worn out by her lack of sleep the previous night and her long day of traveling, Mallory dozed off before they had gotten back on the Northway for the final leg to Hepton Grove. She'd woken up long enough to give Max a weary hug, stumble upstairs to her room, and step out of her clothes and into a set of pajamas before collapsing into bed.

She studied herself in the hall mirror downstairs as she slipped into her charcoal-gray coat. Cassidy's words from last year came to mind: "All gray and black, like she's sad."

Well, she *was* sad, but a bit of color would help hide that fact from any paparazzi who might be lingering in town.

And, with luck, hide it from her family. She would wait until after the holidays to break the news about Gideon.

She grabbed Max's green scarf and looped it around her neck, and then picked up her purse and key ring. It was time to go shopping.

Prescott's pre-Christmas sale was in full swing. Mallory first chose a pair of jeans, and then selected two pairs of dress pants in navy and gray. Next, she purchased several tops: a paisley blouse in shades of emerald and magenta that could be worn with or without the coordinating emerald green jewel-neck sweater; a white blouse with pin stripes of navy, lavender, and rose; and two finely knit turtleneck sweaters, one in teal and one in moss green. A jade green sweater dress and a woven wool-blend skirt and jacket of teal, moss, and gold rounded out her new wardrobe.

Shopping bags in either hand, she was heading towards the revolving door when she felt a hand on her upper arm. She jerked to a halt and, snapping her head to the left, saw Jackson.

"Sorry—I didn't mean to startle you." He smiled dazzlingly. "I was hoping you'd be home for the holidays. Or are you home for good now?"

"Just for the holidays." She looked pointedly at the hand that still gripped her arm. He held it a moment longer and then released it.

"I heard you're dating a celebrity."

"Jackson, what do you want?"

"Well, I was hoping that since you and I are both home for Christmas, we could hang out."

"You're kidding, right?"

"Come on, Mallory. What would it hurt to spend some time together?"

"Our hanging out days ended a long time ago, Jackson. *You* walked out on *me*, remember?"

"I know, and I've regretted it ever since."

She shook her head and started to walk away.

"I want you back, Mallory," he called out.

She stopped, counted to three, and spun on her heel to face him.

"What you want, Jackson, is to try to get another story published. Don't play innocent. I know it was *you* who's responsible for that tabloid somehow getting hold of those pictures of me. That caption calling you the 'discarded fiancé' gave it away. What would the story have been this time—that you've managed to steal me back from Gideon?"

"Mallory, I can explain—"

"You don't need to explain. You sold me out, and you hurt someone I care about very much in the process. We're done." She turned and flounced to the door.

"Guess she finally saw through you, didn't she?" Max said with a grin before following his sister out of the store.

"Hey, Mallory, wait up," Max called, rushing to catch up to her.

"What are you doing here?"

He held up the small Prescott's bag in his hand. "Same thing as you: doing some shopping."

"I guess you heard my run-in with Jackson."

He gave a bark of laughter. "I sure did. It made my day." He reached out and peeked in one of her bags. "It looks like a crayon box exploded. For you?"

She nodded.

"Nice. You know," he said as they walked to Mallory's car, "they're having a winter clothing drive at church. Maybe it's time to give away some of your old clothes."

"I think you're right." She nodded towards the bag he held. "That looks like jewelry or perfume. For someone special?" she asked as she pressed the trunk release button on the key fob.

"Could be," he said, trying to be noncommittal.

"Why, Maxwell Ramsey Glencoe, I believe you're blushing!" she teased as she placed her bags in the trunk.

"I never blush," he retorted. "Want to grab some lunch?"

She closed the trunk lid. "I'd love to."

He reached into his pocket, pulled out a couple of quarters, and fed them into the parking meter. "Let's go."

They walked up the street to Allison's Café and were soon seated at a small table in front of the picture window.

"I'll have the grilled chicken salad with honey mustard on the side, please," Mallory ordered.

"And what to drink?" asked the waitress.

"Just water."

"I'll have the same, but with ranch dressing," Max said, handing both menus to the waitress.

Mallory's phone dinged. She pulled it from her purse. "It's Rachel—Gideon's newest sister-in-law. She's been keeping me posted on what the family's been doing while they're in Branson." She opened the message. "Oh, how cute," she said, turning her phone so Max could see it. "Those are Gabriel's two sons and Graham's daughter on Santa's lap." She scrolled through the pictures. The last one showed the three kids holding their candy canes.

"Hey, isn't that Gideon in the background?" Max asked.

Mallory increased the size of the picture. "Yes it is. It looks like he's talking to Santa."

"Do you mind?" Max asked, taking the phone from her. He increased the picture size some more. "Mal... isn't this the same Santa we saw last year?"

She took back her phone. "Oh my gosh. I think you're right!"

Her phone dinged again. It was a group text from Ethan to all the Lockes and Mallory.

> Important you watch Caitlyn Snow tonight 7 PM ET/6 PM CT.

"What's the matter?"
"Are you going to be home tonight?" she asked.
"Yeah. Why?"
"There's something that you, Mom, and Dad need to see."

———

Bob: Earlier this week, the tabloid Celeb Beat released photos suggesting that Gideon Locke had beaten his girlfriend, Mallory Glencoe. Our own Caitlyn Snow was invited to sit down with Mallory to set the record straight. Her exclusive interview is next.

Caitlyn: Thank you for inviting me to meet with you.

Mallory: Thank you for agreeing to do it on such short notice.

Caitlyn: So, Mallory, are these photos of you real or are they fake?

Mallory: They're very real, Caitlyn.

Caitlyn: Was Gideon Locke responsible for these cuts and bruises on your face?

Mallory: No, not at all. This happened nearly three years ago, long before I met him.

Caitlyn: So what exactly happened?

Mallory: I made the mistake of walking back from the library to my dorm alone late one night. Someone grabbed me and forced me off the sidewalk into the woods.

Caitlyn: Were you raped?

Mallory: No, fortunately there were two couples who had left just minutes after I did, and they found the books and papers I'd dropped. They heard the scuffling in the woods, and they managed to scare off my attacker.

Caitlyn: I see you're shaking even now. That must have been *terribly* traumatic for you.

Mallory: Yes. It was.

Caitlyn: And does Gideon know that you were attacked?

Mallory: Yes he does. I told him not long after we met.

Caitlyn: So he knew about this before these photos were even published?

Mallory: Yes, he did.

Karen Lail

Caitlyn: What was his reaction?

Mallory: Very kind, very understanding, very supportive.

Caitlyn: Now this article also includes a picture of someone that they call your 'discarded fiancé'. Were you, in fact, engaged to him?

Mallory: Yes, we had gotten engaged a few months before the attack.

Caitlyn: How long had you dated before then?

Mallory: About a year.

Caitlyn: So you'd been together almost eighteen months before this happened?

Mallory: Yes.

Caitlyn: What was his reaction?

Mallory: Well, he… Well… He broke off our engagement.

Caitlyn: He broke it off? You didn't?

Mallory: That's right. I did not break it off.

Caitlyn: Why do you think he did that?

Mallory: The attack changed me. I couldn't stand for anyone outside the family to touch me. I didn't want anyone to notice me, so I... I wouldn't leave the house except to go to church or to my parents' eye clinic. And, I felt guilty. *I* was fortunate. Other women who have been in similar situations weren't as lucky, so I didn't think I should have all these fears. It took a long time to get past that.

Caitlyn: So what finally made you heal?

Mallory: It wasn't any one thing. My family helped tremendously, especially Max, my twin brother. He made me laugh again. And then... this is going to sound silly, but last year, Max and I took our niece to see Santa. Santa had a long talk with me in private, encouraging me to go after my dreams. It was pretty much the same thing my family had been saying, but hearing it from someone I didn't know... well, it made me realize it was time to move forward. I had been on pause long enough.

Caitlyn: That's when you came out to Los Angeles?

Mallory: That's right.

Caitlyn: And you met Gideon.

Mallory: Yes. Meeting him also helped me heal.

Caitlyn: How exactly did you meet?

Mallory: We met at a Rams football game. My cousin is dating Ethan Thomas…

Caitlyn: … the son of the Locke Brothers' publicist, Kendra Thomas?

Mallory: Yes… and they had invited me to go with them to the game. Long story short, Gideon was there, too.

Caitlyn: And you've been dating ever since?

Mallory: Yes, as our schedules have allowed. My coursework is demanding and I have a part-time job on campus, and of course he's busy with rehearsals and interviews and performances. But yes, we've dated whenever we could make it work.

Caitlyn: I understand he and his brothers are performing in Branson now. Why didn't you go with them?

Mallory: It was never an option. It's the end of the semester and I had final projects to complete and of course my job. The timing was just off.

Caitlyn: One last question: Are you in love with Gideon Locke, Mallory?

Mallory: Yes, Caitlyn, I'm in love with him.

As the rest of the family cheered over Mallory's closing statement, Gideon pointed the remote and powered off the TV.

She loved him, and she had not said anything about breaking up with him.

It was the best news he'd had in over two weeks.

Karen Lail

CHAPTER 23

"Where are you off to?" Mallory asked, taking in Max's dress pants and plaid dress shirt.

"The clinic. I'm doing an upgrade on the server today. Oh, by the way, Aidan and Phoebe are taking the kids to see Santa tonight. I thought maybe we could all have dinner together first, and then while they go see Santa, you and I could go Christmas caroling with the young adult group afterwards," he suggested as he placed a coffee pod in the Keurig.

"I thought they were going to see Santa tomorrow," Mallory replied, taking a sip of tea.

He positioned a travel mug under the spout and started the brew cycle. "Dad asked Aidan to go to Saratoga for a consultation tomorrow afternoon, and I decided to tag along and see some friends. Aidan's not sure how long it will take, so he and Phoebe decided to take the kids tonight."

"Sure, I'll go. What time?"

"Right after the clinic closes. Christmas caroling starts at seven."

"Okay, I'll meet you at the clinic at five."

"Sounds good. So what are you doing today?"

"I'm going to run a couple of errands for Mom. I thought I'd also do some Christmas shopping and maybe pick up some toys for the toy drive, too. Mom reminded me that the church Christmas party is on Saturday."

Max drew out his wallet and handed over two twenties. "Here, pick up…"

"… an extra toy," they finished in unison.

Mallory took the money from him. "Wow, talk about déja-vu."

He handed over two more bills before tucking his wallet back in his pocket. "Well then, make it *two* extra toys, please."

"I'll be glad to."

"Thanks. And be careful. After last night's interview, I wouldn't be surprised if reporters start showing up in town again." The Keurig sputtered, signaling the end of the brew cycle. He discarded the pod and snapped the lid on his mug. "Gotta go—you know what task-masters my bosses are," he said with a grin.

They confronted her as she exited Carson's Bakery, where she had placed an order for twelve dozen cupcakes for pick-up on Saturday morning. They trailed her to the library, where she returned a book for her mother. They swarmed around her as she walked down to Prescott's.

Keep your head up and just keep walking.

She stopped suddenly. A new business had opened next to Ful-bright Insurance. She studied the sign a moment longer and then, pulling out her phone and dialing a number, she resumed walking toward the department store.

"Hello, Lettie? I have an idea that I want to talk over with you…"

The number of paparazzi had dwindled by the time she left Prescott's. The temperature had dropped, and occasional large snow-flakes spiraled from the sky. When she reached the clinic, the snow-fall was steady, the cold penetrating. She hurried around to the staff parking lot where she had left her car, and deposited her shopping bags in the trunk before slipping through the staff entrance.

Passing Aidan's office, she stopped in the doorway of her parents' office. Cassidy and baby Jeremy were seated on Roger's lap and he was slowly rotating his chair, first to the left, then to the right.

Mallory smiled. "I see you're starting Jeremy off right."

"Did you have any doubts?" Roger said with an answering grin.

"He's drooling, Mommy," Cassidy pointed out. "It's disgusting."

Phoebe laughed as she bent down to wipe a string of slobber from the baby's mouth. "It's okay, Cassidy. You did the same thing when you were teething."

Max joined Mallory in the doorway. "The reporters are back."

"Yes, I'm afraid they followed me from Prescott's." Her eyes swept from Max to Meredythe, Aidan, Phoebe, and Roger. "Why don't you guys go ahead and get a table and I'll be along in a few minutes? I can lock up."

"Are you sure you want to face them alone?" Meredythe asked doubtfully.

"I've been doing it all day."

"No, I'm staying with you," Max said, his voice firm.

"All right."

Minutes later, the twins watched the rest of the family exit the clinic, and then they did the final sweep of the building: making sure all the restrooms were empty of visitors; checking the power settings on the equipment; ensuring the medical records room, display cases, desks, and the front door were secured.

"You ready?" Max asked as he shrugged into his coat.

Mallory adjusted a setting on her phone. "Just about. There's something I need to do real quick."

> I know tonight is your last performance in
> Branson. Hope it goes well.

Branson, MO

Gideon and his family were sharing an early dinner when his phone dinged. *Mallory.* Hope burgeoning, he read the message and smiled as he typed.

> Thanks. I miss you.

Better not press my luck. He erased the last sentence and pressed Send.

CHAPTER 24

Saturday, December 14ᵗʰ

Hepton Grove

"Is this the last of it?" Max asked, lifting the box of clothing from the desk and turning towards the doorway.

Mallory reached around him and placed one more folded black sweatshirt in the box. "Now it is."

"Wow, I'm proud of you. You cleared out a lot."

"It was time," she stated as she followed him out of her room.

Roger and Meredythe were waiting for them at the bottom of the stairs. Roger held the box while Max and Mallory pulled their coats from the closet.

"All set?" Roger asked, handing the box back to Max as Mallory picked up a large shopping bag.

"I've got the clothes, and Mallory has the toys, so…" He looked at Mallory, who nodded. "… We're ready."

―――――――――

Upon entering the fellowship hall, Roger, Meredythe, and Mallory placed toys in the "Hepton Grove Annual Toy Drive" bin while Max set the box next to a container labeled "Clothing Drive".

"Welcome," Pastor Dan greeted, grasping hands with each of them.

"This is quite a turnout," Roger remarked.

"It's our largest crowd yet."

Max touched the sleeve of Mallory's jade green sweater dress. "Come on—let's go scope out the competition."

"We have a couple of new games this year that you may want to check out," Pastor Dan called after them. Grinning, Max held up a thumb before turning away.

Cassidy pirouetted in front of them, one upraised hand clutching a half-eaten candy cane. She suddenly angled toward Max.

"Whoa, missy," he said, grabbing her shoulders and holding her at arm's length. "You're dangerous with that thing!"

Cassidy looked up at him. "Sorry, Uncle Max. I got a little dizzy."

He stooped down to face her. "Well, I have an idea. Why don't you finish eating your candy cane, and by then you won't be dizzy anymore."

"Okay!"

He patted her shoulder and stood up.

"Disaster averted," Max murmured as he and Mallory continued towards the games section.

"Your public thanks you," she said, bringing her hand up in front of her right shoulder for a subtle high-five.

Max scanned the crowd. "I don't want to freak you out, but I think a couple of your paparazzi are here."

"Well, it *is* a community party. As long as they don't bother us, I don't have any problem with them being here."

"Who are you, and what have you done with my sister?" he teased.

She reached up and shoved his shoulder playfully.

"Ah, *now* I recognize you," said Max.

"Hi, Max," a female voice greeted.

The twins looked to their left.

"There you are!" Max exclaimed, hugging the petite blonde. "I was afraid you'd changed your mind about coming!"

She smiled up at him. "No, we just stopped off to pick up some toys for your toy drive. It took longer to check out than we anticipated."

"We?"

"Harper wanted to come, too."

Mallory watched as an odd expression flitted across Max's face. *Harper. Wasn't that the girl who had texted Max twice last year after their visit to Santa?*

"Oh. Well, I'm glad you could make it," Max said. "Lacey, this is my sister, Mallory. Mallory, this is my friend, Lacey Rollins."

"It's nice to meet you," Mallory said, extending her hand.

Lacey grasped it. "You too."

"Lacey was part of the group that went with me on the ski trip to Colorado last year," Max explained. "We've gone skiing a couple of times since then."

"Oh, nice." She looked between Max and Lacey. "Well, Max, why don't you take Lacey to check out the games? I'm going to get something to drink. I'll catch up with you later."

Max looked at Lacey questioningly.

"Sounds great," she agreed.

Tossing a grateful smile at his sister, Max took Lacey's elbow and guided her towards the other side of the fellowship hall.

Mallory looked after them for a moment and then turned in the opposite direction. As she headed towards the refreshment table, she noticed all the couples, both old and young, who were milling around, laughing and chatting. She waved to her parents, who were talking to the Wyatts, and then to Aidan and Phoebe, who were helping baby Jeremy place his hand in a small round mold filled with plaster of Paris. She looked again at Max and with a pang realized he was preparing for the Three-Legged Present Dash with Lacey as his partner.

Suddenly, she felt an overwhelming need to escape.

The pendant lights had been dimmed to their lowest setting and the large stained glass cross that took up most of the wall above the choir alcove was backlit by the street lamps outside. Mallory made her way down the aisle to her family's usual pew: left side, third row from the front. She sank down on the padded bench and leaned against the back, the coolness of the wood seeping through her dress.

She focused on the cross and silently named her troubles and her blessings. It was one of the practices that had sustained her during those eighteen months following the assault.

Before she had gone to Los Angeles. Before she had met Gideon.

Gideon. He lay heaviest on her heart. She should never have let their last night together end as it had. She'd been caught off guard, and instead of responding quietly and rationally to his accusations, she'd allowed the situation to escalate until she'd said words that she now regretted.

She thought of the message she'd sent to him on Thursday. She'd intended it as an olive branch of sorts, but Gideon's curt reply burned in her mind. It could only mean he was upset with her still. After all, she had walked away from him, blocked him out.

Who does that to someone they profess to love?

But surprisingly, there had been no word from Rachel since the pictures from their visit to Santa. Mallory had half expected a message after the interview with Caitlyn Snow had aired, but there was only silence.

Perhaps they hadn't seen the interview. Perhaps they were too busy getting ready for one of their performances to watch it.

But that wouldn't explain why Rachel's daily updates had ceased completely.

Unless they *had* seen the interview and were all outraged by the things she'd said.

Like not making it clear that she had broken up with Gideon.

Like claiming she loved him.

She buried her face in her hands and pleaded to have the burden of guilt, of regret, of overwhelming loss to be lifted from her.

After a time, she lowered her hands, lifted her head, and rose from the pew. She knew her next course of action. When she returned to Los Angeles in January she would reach out to him one final time.

With one last glance at the cross, she went back up the aisle and, pushing open one of the double doors, walked out of the sanctuary.

Straight into Gideon.

———

He reached out to steady her. "Are you all right?"

"Yes." She reached out and smoothed a collar point on Gideon's shirt that had been knocked askew by the collision. Afraid the intimate gesture had overstepped, she drew back her hand. "Sorry," she said at the same time he said, "Thank you."

"Could we sit and talk in private somewhere?" he continued.

Mallory pointed to the double doors behind her. He opened one of the doors and motioned for her to lead the way.

He looked up at the vaulted ceiling, side to side at the evenly spaced arched stained glass windows, and then ahead at the cross as he followed Mallory down the aisle. "What a beautiful church," he remarked as they settled in the pew Mallory had vacated just moments ago.

She nodded, looking at the cross. "It's been a place of love and security and refuge for most of my life."

A heavy silence fell between them. After a moment, eyes still fixed on the cross, Mallory asked, "What brought you to Hepton Grove, Gideon? And how did you know I would be here, at the church?"

He answered the last question first. "Your dad told me you'd be here for the party."

Mallory turned her head in shock.

"Rachel told you we all took the kids to see Santa last week, right?"

She nodded.

"It turns out it was the same Santa I'd met on a street corner in Los Angeles last year. He'd given me some good advice back then, so I stayed and chatted with him for a few minutes after the kids were done," he continued. "And then I called your dad at his office and asked if I could take him up on his offer to come for a visit. I told him everything about that last night at your apartment, about how I'd acted, how wrong I'd been, how I wanted to ask your forgiveness in person."

"I guess Dad was surprised. I hadn't told my family about what happened between us."

"Yes, that's what he said—and that surprised *me*. I figured as close as you are to your family, you would have told them… if not that night, then as soon as you flew home."

"I was going to, but I didn't want to ruin the holidays." *And thank goodness I didn't tell them*, she thought. *Max might have felt obligated to stay with me tonight instead of spending time with Lacey.*

"Anyway, your dad told me I could come, but he suggested I stay in a hotel in Saratoga Springs last night. He arranged for Max and

Aidan to pick me up at the airport yesterday after some meeting they had, and they dropped me off at the hotel on their way home. I thought it was best not to try to see you until the party. When I couldn't find you, your parents pointed me this way." He looked at her earnestly. "Can you forgive me?"

She shifted slightly to face him, her words coming out in a rush. "That last night… I handled everything badly. I should never have walked away… I should have stayed until I convinced you that—"

He stayed her with a touch of his hand. "It was my fault, first to last."

She shook her head. "It takes two to argue."

"Hmmm, sounds like something my parents said to my brothers and me."

She chuckled. "Mine too."

He took hold of both of her hands. "*Can* you forgive me?" he repeated.

"If you can forgive me."

"I can. I do."

"Me too."

Slowly he bent forward to kiss her, releasing her hands only to wrap his arms around her.

"Oh, I've missed you," he said, nuzzling her ear, breathing deeply of her scent.

"I've missed you, too." She drew back to face him. "I've missed *us.*"

They lapsed into silence again, this time comfortably.

"So tell me: how did Kendra convince you to do that interview?"

"She didn't—it was my idea. I just asked her to set it up for me."

"*You*—camera-shy Mallory—*asked* to be interviewed by Caitlyn Snow?"

She laughed. "I know—it's crazy. But when Lettie showed me that tabloid and all those pictures they'd gotten hold of, I knew I needed to set the record straight. I remembered you saying Caitlyn at least *tries* to get the story right, so I asked Kendra to arrange the interview with her—and only her."

"I'm amazed." He glanced at the cross, considering his next words, but she forestalled him.

"I meant every word, Gideon," she said softly. "Every one."

He didn't pretend to misunderstand. "I love you, too, Mallory. I wanted to tell you that the last night we were together." He bent and kissed her gently. "I know you think it's complicated for us. I know you plan to move back here when you graduate."

She laughed and drew out her phone. "There's something I've got to show you. I talked to Lettie and we're going to be partners. Look." She held out her phone to show him the mock-up of a sign.

Glencoe Architectural Design
Residential | Commercial | Historic Preservation
Saratoga Springs, NY | Los Angeles, CA

"Saratoga Springs *and* Los Angeles? Really?"

"Uh huh. I'd still want to live *here* in Hepton Grove, but it's an easy commute to Saratoga. And because of you, Los Angeles is like a second home to me now."

That prompted another kiss.

"There's something I need to tell you, too. While we were in Branson, Gabriel went to Dad and asked him to call a family meeting. The upshot is that Gabriel and Courtney want us to scale back on our performances after our summer tour. Jesse will be starting kindergarten next fall, and Gabriel and Courtney both want to be involved with his school. So when my brothers and I aren't rehearsing or recording or performing, I can be with you, wherever you are."

"Really?"

"Really." He looked at her earnestly. "But if we take that step, Mallory, I want to be totally up front with the public about our relationship. I want the world to know that we're not just dating casually—you're my girlfriend."

"So you're asking me to go steady with you?" she teased.

He laughed. "If you want to call it that, then yes." He paused for one, two, three beats, and when she didn't say anything, he asked, "So what do you say?"

She stood up and then bent down to grab his hand. "Before I

commit to anything, let's see how you are at the Three-Legged Present Dash."

He rose and led her out of the pew and up the aisle, saying, "I'll have you know, I'm awesome at the Three-Legged Present Dash—as long as you're my partner."

Karen Lail

EPILOGUE

One Year Later

Hepton Grove

"It's a very cold gray December day here in Hepton Grove, New York, where in less than twenty minutes entertainer Gideon Locke will marry his longtime girlfriend, Mallory Glencoe, in this church," the reporter from one of the local network affiliates said to the camera, gesturing to the building behind her. "We've been told the bride and groom will each have just one attendant. Gareth Locke, Gideon's youngest brother, will serve as best man. The bride's cousin and business partner, Letitia Glencoe Thomas, is matron of honor. Wedding guests are limited to the bride and groom's extended family and a few close friends, including publicist Kendra Thomas and her husband, Bill. Yet as you can see," she continued, stepping to one side as the camera slowly panned, "many of the local townspeople—and even Santa Claus—have gathered across the street from the church, hoping to catch a glimpse of the bride and groom as they depart for their reception…"

"It's time," Pastor Dan said with a grin.

Gareth clapped Gideon on the back, and the brothers shared a smile as they followed Pastor Dan through the door and into the chancel area. Assuming his position, Gideon took note of the small tables that flanked the steps to the altar. Each table held four lighted white pillar candles, nestled among seasonal greenery: one candle for each of Mallory's and Gideon's grandparents.

He watched Garrison walk down the aisle alone and enter the first pew on the groom's side, where a framed picture of Grace was positioned, a single red rose laying in front of it. Next, Max escorted Meredythe to the front of the sanctuary. Once she sat down, he took his place on the second pew where Lacey, Aidan, Phoebe, Cassidy, and Jeremy were seated.

Silently, Gideon counted the heavy downbeats of "Carol of the Bells" and waited for the processional. He smiled inwardly, recalling the struggle they'd had choosing the song that would bring Mallory to the altar. Since Pachelbel's "Canon in D" had been used by Rachel and Gareth, and again for Lettie and Ethan's wedding, Mallory was adamant about selecting something different. Gideon had suggested they choose something seasonal, and Mallory had latched on to that idea, deciding in that moment to make *all* their wedding music Christmas-themed. The songs for the prelude and recessional were easy to choose, but the processional… The organist had suggested using "Carol of the Bells" both to chime the hour *and* process, but when Mallory tried walking in time to the accented beats, she said she felt like she was marching. She wanted something more lilting, something she could walk more naturally to. Desperate, she had roped Gideon into watching the wedding scenes of what seemed like every Hallmark Christmas movie for ideas. At last they agreed on "Bring a Torch, Jeanette, Isabella," the strains of which were now starting. He turned eagerly.

Lettie, in a flowing dress of soft green and holding a nosegay of greenery and white and deep pink flowers tied with a chocolate-colored ribbon, walked towards the altar and took her place opposite Gareth and Gideon. Meredythe stood up, and the rest of the guests rose as well.

And there she was, the love of his life, her hand tucked in her father's arm. Gideon drank in every detail: the simple but elegant wedding dress that molded to her shape; the two-tiered veil whose edges glistened with delicate crystals; the earrings of emeralds and diamonds—his wedding gift to her; the bouquet of assorted white flowers, supple greenery, and pinecones dipped in gold or silver and dotted with crystals.

Karen Lail

"Breathe," Gareth whispered to him.

Tossing a grin, he stepped down and, with ineffable tenderness, took the hand of his bride.

―――――――――――

As they headed to the double doors of the sanctuary, the recording of "Christmas in the Key of G" played over the sound system, the words and music seeming to buoy them along as they walked out of the church and down the steps to the waiting limousine. Cameras flashed and friends and neighbors cheered.

A crisp ring of a bell caught Gideon's attention as the chauffeur held the door open. Gideon searched the crowd. Yes, there, on the far street corner, was the Santa he'd met two years ago. Their eyes met, and Gideon smiled and nodded before turning his attention back to helping Mallory into the car.

Gideon sighed and slipped his arm around Mallory's shoulders as the chauffeur slowly guided the limousine away from the curb.

"You know, I've been thinking: maybe I should change the title of that song to 'Christmas in the Key of We'."

"No," replied Mallory, laying her hand on his thigh. "That song will always be for your mom. We'll write our own song."

He stroked the side of her face. "Yes, we will." He leaned down and kissed her.

―――――――――――

The crowd dispersed, but Santa remained where he was, watching the limousine travel to the end of the road, turn right, and pass out of sight. With a satisfied smile, he gently set the bell on top of the donation pail. Then, with a quick look around to make sure he was alone, he placed a finger aside of his nose.

And vanished.

ABOUT THE AUTHOR

Karen Lail grew up in Upstate New York in small towns not too different from fictional Hepton Grove. A former technical writer for a national bank, she now resides with her husband in yet another small town in North Carolina.

CPSIA information can be obtained
at www.ICGtesting.com
Printed in the USA
LVHW050731171120
671903LV00004B/204